God's
Love
for
You

God's Love for You

Hannah Whitall Smith

Whitaker House

GOD'S LOVE FOR YOU

ISBN: 0-88368-529-9
Printed in the United States of America
Copyright © 1999 by Whitaker House

Whitaker House
30 Hunt Valley Circle
New Kensington, PA 15068

Library of Congress Cataloging-in-Publication Data

Smith, Hannah Whitall, 1832–1911.
    God's love for you / by Hannah Whitall Smith.—[Rev. ed.].
       p. cm.
    Rev. ed. of.: The open secret. 1885.
    ISBN 0-88368-529-9 (pbk.)
    1. Christian life—Biblical teaching—Miscellanea. I. Smith,
Hannah Whitall, 1832–1911. Open secret. II. Title.

BS680.C47 S57 1999
248.4—dc21   99-040095

1 2 3 4 5 6 7 8 9 10 11 12 13 /11 10 09 08 07 06 05 04 03 02 01 00

Contents

Introduction

In this book are ten Bible lessons that I have prepared for you. However, in this introduction, I would like to present an effective method of preparing your own Bible lessons. To follow this method, you will need four things:

1. A Bible—with cross-references, if possible.

2. *Cruden's Complete Concordance* or *Young's Analytical Concordance.*

3. A notebook.

4. An undisturbed desk or table where you can keep the above three things, along with a supply of pens, always ready.

After obtaining these few necessary things, proceed as follows:

1. Commit yourself to the Lord with a few words of prayer, asking for light and guidance and expecting to receive them.

2. Choose a subject appropriate to the occasion.

3. In the concordance, find all the words referring to this subject. From among the texts given, select those that seem to best shed light on the subject, listing them in your notebook.

4. Read over the selected texts carefully, and make a list of the most striking ones on a separate piece of paper. To put them in the order that will best develop the lesson, begin your list with a familiar text and gradually progress to those not so well-known, letting each successive text develop the subject a little more clearly than the last. Conclude the list, if possible, with some practical instance from Bible history, or some biblical illustration that includes a type. (I will explain more about types in Chapter 6.)

5. After preparing your list, open your Bible to the first text, and in the margin beside it, write the reference to the second text on your list. Turn to this second one, and write beside it the reference to the third. Turn to the third, and write beside it the reference to the fourth, and so on through the whole list. Finally, refer to your first text, the foundation text, and sum up the whole subject.

6. On a blank page at the end of your Bible, write down an index of all the subjects you have studied in this way, along with the foundation text for each subject. If you have no blank pages at

the end of your Bible, tape a half sheet of note-book paper inside the back cover.

7. If you want, you can write a list of all your texts in the margin beside the first text, so that you have them all in front of you at once to choose from.

8. By this plan, you will have a complete chain of texts on any given subject running through your Bible, each verse referring you to the next one that you should read. This method avoids the trouble of loose slips of paper, which could easily cause you embarrassment by falling out of your Bible. Also, having once studied a subject, you will have it ready for any future use. By turning to your index, you can, at a moment's notice, open your Bible to the foundation text, and then turn to one text after another throughout the whole course of your lesson, without hesitation or uneasiness.

Chapter 1

Our Savior

Then the angel said to them, "Do not be afraid,
for behold, I bring you good tidings of great
joy which will be to all people. For there is born to
you this day in the city of David a Savior,
who is Christ the Lord."
—Luke 2:10–11

Notice that Christ is "a Savior," not a Helper; that is, He is One who saves, not merely One who offers to help us save ourselves. He knows our helplessness and therefore declared that He had come "to seek and to save."

[Jesus said,] "The Son of Man has come to seek and to save that which was lost."   LUKE 19:10

"I am with you to save you and deliver you," says the LORD.   JEREMIAH 15:20

WHO IS THIS SAVIOR?

I am the LORD your God, the Holy One of Israel, your Savior....I, even I, am the LORD, and besides Me there is no savior.   ISAIAH 43:3, 11

There is no other God besides Me, a just God and a Savior; there is none besides Me....Look to Me, and be saved, all you ends of the earth! For I am God, and there is no other.   ISAIAH 45:21–22

The God who created us is the God who saves us. Not another god, for there is none besides Him, but the very God our Creator Himself. Some are prone to think of our Creator and our Savior as two Gods, with interests that are not identical. But we are told as plainly as words can tell it that the Creator is also the Savior, and "there is none besides."

To God our Savior, who alone is wise, be glory and majesty, dominion and power, both now and forever. Amen.   JUDE 25

You shall know that I, the LORD, am your Savior and your Redeemer, the Mighty One of Jacob.
ISAIAH 60:16

For to this end we both labor and suffer reproach, because we trust in the living God, who is the Savior of all men, especially of those who believe.
1 TIMOTHY 4:10

And without controversy great is the mystery of godliness: God was manifested in the flesh, justified in the Spirit, seen by angels, preached among the Gentiles, believed on in the world, received up in glory.   1 TIMOTHY 3:16

Therefore, since it is God, the almighty God, the Creator of heaven and earth, who is our Savior, there can be no question about His ability to save us.

We may rest our case in His care without any anxiety or fear.

FROM WHAT DOES GOD SAVE US?

He saves us from our sins.

And she will bring forth a Son, and you shall call
His name JESUS, for He will save His people from
their sins.   MATTHEW 1:21

To you first, God, having raised up His Servant
Jesus, sent Him to bless you, in turning away
every one of you from your iniquities.   ACTS 3:26

Who gave Himself for us, that He might redeem us
from every lawless deed and purify for Himself His
own special people, zealous for good works.
                                                        TITUS 2:14

He saves us from our temptations.

For in that He Himself has suffered, being
tempted, He is able to aid those who are tempted.
                                                    HEBREWS 2:18

No temptation has overtaken you except such as is
common to man; but God is faithful, who will not
allow you to be tempted beyond what you are able,
but with the temptation will also make the way of
escape, that you may be able to bear it.
                                          1 CORINTHIANS 10:13

He saves us from our cares.

Casting all your care upon Him, for He cares for you.   1 PETER 5:7

Be anxious for nothing, but in everything by prayer and supplication, with thanksgiving, let your requests be made known to God; and the peace of God, which surpasses all understanding, will guard your hearts and minds through Christ Jesus.   PHILIPPIANS 4:6–7

He saves us from our troubles.

You are my hiding place; You shall preserve me from trouble; You shall surround me with songs of deliverance.   PSALM 32:7

He saves us from our bondage to sin and Satan.

Thus says the LORD: "...For now I will break off his yoke from you, and burst your bonds apart."
                                    NAHUM 1:12–13

O LORD, truly I am Your servant; I am Your servant, the son of Your maidservant; You have loosed my bonds.   PSALM 116:16

He saves us from our enemies.

Blessed is the Lord God of Israel, for He has visited and redeemed His people, and has raised up a horn of salvation for us in the house of His servant David, as He spoke by the mouth of His holy prophets, who have been since the world began, that we should be saved from our enemies and from the hand of all who hate us, to perform the mercy promised to our fathers and to remember His holy covenant, the oath which He swore to our father Abraham: to grant us that we, being delivered from the hand of our enemies, might serve Him without fear, in holiness and righteousness before Him all the days of our life.   LUKE 1:68–75

He saves us from our fears.

I sought the LORD, and He heard me, and delivered me from all my fears.   PSALM 34:4

You shall not be afraid of the terror by night, nor of the arrow that flies by day, nor of the pestilence that walks in darkness, nor of the destruction that lays waste at noonday.   PSALM 91:5–6

Inasmuch then as the children have partaken of flesh and blood, He Himself likewise shared in the same, that through death He might destroy him who had the power of death, that is, the devil, and release those who through fear of death were all their lifetime subject to bondage.
                                    HEBREWS 2:14–15

This does not mean that we will have no temptations to entice us, no cares to burden us, no enemies to attack us, no sorrows to grieve us. But out of them all, and in them all, we will be saved with an interior salvation that will continually make us "more than conquerors" (Romans 8:37).

WHOM DOES GOD SAVE?

He saves those who are lost.

[Jesus said,] "For the Son of Man has come to save that which was lost."   MATTHEW 18:11

For thus says the Lord GOD: "Indeed I Myself will search for My sheep and seek them out. As a shepherd seeks out his flock on the day he is among his scattered sheep, so will I seek out My sheep and deliver them from all the places where they were scattered on a cloudy and dark day....I will seek what was lost and bring back what was driven away, bind up the broken and strengthen what was sick."   EZEKIEL 34:11–12, 16

So He spoke this parable to them, saying: "What man of you, having a hundred sheep, if he loses one of them, does not leave the ninety-nine in the wilderness, and go after the one which is lost until he finds it?"   LUKE 15:3–4

He saves sinners—bad people who feel themselves to be unworthy.

This is a faithful saying and worthy of all acceptance, that Christ Jesus came into the world to save sinners, of whom I am chief.   1 TIMOTHY 1:15

[Jesus said,] "I have not come to call the righteous, but sinners, to repentance."   LUKE 5:32

Also He spoke this parable to some who trusted in themselves that they were righteous, and despised others: "Two men went up to the temple to pray, one a Pharisee and the other a tax collector. The Pharisee stood and prayed thus with himself, 'God, I thank You that I am not like other men; extortioners, unjust, adulterers, or even as this tax collector. I fast twice a week; I give tithes of all that I possess.' And the tax collector, standing afar off, would not so much as raise his eyes to heaven, but beat his breast, saying, 'God, be merciful to me a sinner!' I tell you, this man went down to his house justified rather than the other; for everyone who exalts himself will be humbled, and he who humbles himself will be exalted."   LUKE 18:9–14

He saves the helpless.

And He said to me, "My grace is sufficient for you, for My strength is made perfect in weakness."
                                           2 CORINTHIANS 12:9

He gives power to the weak, and to those who have no might He increases strength.   ISAIAH 40:29

He saves the spiritually sick.

When Jesus heard that, He said to them, "Those who are well have no need of a physician, but those who are sick."   MATTHEW 9:12

He saves the world.

And He Himself is the propitiation for our sins, and not for ours only but also for the whole world.
                                           1 JOHN 2:2

And we have seen and testify that the Father has sent the Son as Savior of the world.   1 JOHN 4:14

Then they said to the woman, "Now we believe, not because of what you said, for we ourselves have heard Him and we know that this is indeed the Christ, the Savior of the world."   JOHN 4:42

HOW DID GOD ANNOUNCE HIS OWN MISSION WHEN ON EARTH?

So He came to Nazareth, where He had been brought up. And as His custom was, He went into the synagogue on the Sabbath day, and stood up to read. And He was handed the book of the prophet Isaiah. And when He had opened the book, He found the place where it was written: "The Spirit of the LORD is upon Me, because He has anointed Me to preach the gospel to the poor; He has sent Me to heal the brokenhearted, to proclaim liberty to the captives and recovery of sight to the blind, to set at liberty those who are oppressed; to proclaim the acceptable year of the LORD." Then He closed the book, and gave it back to the attendant and sat down. And the eyes of all who were in the synagogue were fixed on Him. And He began to say to them, "Today this Scripture is fulfilled in your hearing."   LUKE 4:16–21

WHEN DOES GOD SAVE US?

He saves NOW.

Behold, now is the accepted time; behold, now is the day of salvation.   2 CORINTHIANS 6:2

God is our refuge and strength, a very present help in trouble.   PSALM 46:1

HOW DOES GOD SAVE US?

By His own mighty power, and out of His own heart of love and mercy.

For they did not gain possession of the land by their own sword, nor did their own arm save them; but it was Your right hand, Your arm, and the light of Your countenance, because You favored them.   PSALM 44:3

Not by works of righteousness which we have done, but according to His mercy He saved us, through the washing of regeneration and renewing of the Holy Spirit.   TITUS 3:5

For by grace you have been saved through faith, and that not of yourselves; it is the gift of God, not of works, lest anyone should boast.
                                          EPHESIANS 2:8–9

And Moses said to the people, "Do not be afraid. Stand still, and see the salvation of the LORD, which He will accomplish for you today. For the Egyptians whom you see today, you shall see again no more forever. The LORD will fight for you, and you shall hold your peace."   EXODUS 14:13–14

WHY DOES GOD SAVE US?

Because He loves us.

[Jesus said,] "For God so loved the world that He gave His only begotten Son, that whoever believes in Him should not perish but have everlasting life." JOHN 3:16

In this the love of God was manifested toward us, that God has sent His only begotten Son into the world, that we might live through Him.

1 JOHN 4:9

[God] has saved us and called us with a holy calling, not according to our works, but according to His own purpose and grace which was given to us in Christ Jesus before time began, but has now been revealed by the appearing of our Savior Jesus Christ, who has abolished death and brought life and immortality to light through the gospel.

2 TIMOTHY 1:9–10

Also, He saves us in order to show forth to the universe the exceeding riches of His grace, and of His wisdom and His power.

But God, who is rich in mercy, because of His great love with which He loved us, even when we were dead in trespasses, made us alive together with Christ (by grace you have been saved), and raised us up together, and made us sit together in the heavenly places in Christ Jesus, that in the ages to come He might show the exceeding riches of His grace in His kindness toward us in Christ Jesus. EPHESIANS 2:4–7

To the intent that now the manifold wisdom of God might be made known by the church to the principalities and powers in the heavenly places.

EPHESIANS 3:10

WHAT IS OUR PART IN THIS SALVATION?

The part that we play in our salvation is three-fold: surrender, trust, and obedience.

Surrender

Therefore submit to God. Resist the devil and he will flee from you.   JAMES 4:7

O You who hear prayer, to You all flesh will come.
PSALM 65:2

Incline your ear, and come to Me. Hear, and your soul shall live; and I will make an everlasting covenant with you; the sure mercies of David.
ISAIAH 55:3

[Jesus said,] "Come to Me, all you who labor and are heavy laden, and I will give you rest."
MATTHEW 11:28

But as for me, I would seek God, and to God I would commit my cause.   JOB 5:8

Seek the LORD while He may be found, call upon Him while He is near. Let the wicked forsake his way, and the unrighteous man his thoughts; let him return to the LORD, and He will have mercy on him; and to our God, for He will abundantly pardon.   ISAIAH 55:6–7

Therefore "Come out from among them and be separate, says the Lord. Do not touch what is unclean, and I will receive you." "I will be a Father to you, and you shall be My sons and daughters, says the LORD Almighty." 2 CORINTHIANS 6:17–18

Therefore let those who suffer according to the will of God commit their souls to Him in doing good, as to a faithful Creator. 1 PETER 4:19

Trust

But without faith it is impossible to please Him, for he who comes to God must believe that He is, and that He is a rewarder of those who diligently seek Him. HEBREWS 11:6

Commit your way to the LORD, trust also in Him, and He shall bring it to pass. PSALM 37:5

Some trust in chariots, and some in horses; but we will remember the name of the LORD our God. They have bowed down and fallen; but we have risen and stand upright. PSALM 20:7–8

And the LORD shall help them and deliver them; He shall deliver them from the wicked, and save them, because they trust in Him. PSALM 37:40

Those who trust in the LORD are like Mount Zion, which cannot be moved, but abides forever. PSALM 125:1

But what does it say? "The word is near you, in your mouth and in your heart" (that is, the word of faith which we preach): that if you confess with your mouth the Lord Jesus and believe in your heart that God has raised Him from the dead, you will be saved. For with the heart one believes unto righteousness, and with the mouth confession is made unto salvation. For the Scripture says, "Whoever believes on Him will not be put to shame." For there is no distinction between Jew and Greek, for the same Lord over all is rich to all who call upon Him. For "whoever calls on the name of the LORD shall be saved."

ROMANS 10:8–13

[Jesus said,] "And as Moses lifted up the serpent in the wilderness, even so must the Son of Man be lifted up, that whoever believes in Him should not perish but have eternal life."   JOHN 3:14–15

[Jesus said,] "Most assuredly, I say to you, he who believes in Me has everlasting life."   JOHN 6:47

[Jesus said,] "And this is the will of Him who sent Me, that everyone who sees the Son and believes in Him may have everlasting life; and I will raise him up at the last day."   JOHN 6:40

To Him all the prophets witness that, through His name, whoever believes in Him will receive remission of sins.   ACTS 10:43

Therefore let it be known to you, brethren, that through this Man is preached to you the forgiveness of sins; and by Him everyone who believes is justified from all things from which you could not be justified by the law of Moses.   ACTS 13:38–39

Obedience

Do you not know that to whom you present yourselves slaves to obey, you are that one's slaves

whom you obey, whether of sin leading to death, or
of obedience leading to righteousness?

ROMANS 6:16

[Jesus said,] "Not everyone who says to Me, 'Lord,
Lord,' shall enter the kingdom of heaven, but he
who does the will of My Father in heaven. Many
will say to Me in that day, 'Lord, Lord, have we
not prophesied in Your name, cast out demons in
Your name, and done many wonders in Your
name?' And then I will declare to them, 'I never
knew you; depart from Me, you who practice law-
lessness!' Therefore whoever hears these sayings
of Mine, and does them, I will liken him to a wise
man who built his house on the rock: and the rain
descended, the floods came, and the winds blew
and beat on that house; and it did not fall, for it
was founded on the rock. But everyone who hears
these sayings of Mine, and does not do them, will
be like a foolish man who built his house on the
sand: and the rain descended, the floods came, and
the winds blew and beat on that house; and it fell.
And great was its fall." MATTHEW 7:21–27

But be doers of the word, and not hearers only, de-
ceiving yourselves. JAMES 1:22

What does it profit, my brethren, if someone says
he has faith but does not have works? Can faith
save him?...Thus also faith by itself, if it does not
have works, is dead....For as the body without the
spirit is dead, so faith without works is dead also.

JAMES 2:14, 17, 26

Not one of these three things—surrender, trust,
or obedience—will do without the others. Not only

must we yield ourselves utterly to God, but we must also trust Him. Furthermore, we must walk in obedience to Him. I believe that it is impossible to do any one of these three things fully without doing the others also, for they are inseparably connected. We cannot yield unless we trust, and we cannot trust unless we both yield and obey. Just as fire without heat is an impossibility, so faith without works is an impossibility. There is no contradiction, therefore, between the teachings of Paul, who emphasized faith, and James, who emphasized works. These two Bible writers were only developing different sides of the same truth—equally essential sides.

What must we do to make Christ our Savior?

We can do nothing to *make* Him our Savior, for He has already been *born* our Savior. The announcement of the angels was, "There is born to you this day in the city of David a Savior, who is Christ the Lord" (Luke 2:11). All we can do, therefore, is to believe this announcement and to receive Him as our Savior.

When a little brother is born into a family, the other children do not ask, "What should we do to make him our brother?" On the contrary, they joyfully announce to all who enter the house, "Oh, we have a little brother! We have a new little brother! Don't you want to see him?"

Let us be like them in the simplicity of our faith. Believing the declaration that a Savior has been born unto us, let us tell everyone the joyful news.

Chapter 2

God Is Love

He who does not love does not know God,
for God is love.
—1 John 4:8

Notice that the above verse does not say merely that God is loving, but that "God is love." That is, love is His very nature, His essence. Love is not merely one of His attributes, but it is Himself. Therefore, all that He does is from the root of love. No matter how our circumstances may look, we must believe this fact, because it cannot be otherwise.

Behold what manner of love the Father has bestowed on us, that we should be called children of God! Therefore the world does not know us, because it did not know Him.   1 JOHN 3:1

We are to behold the "manner of love," that is, the sort or kind of love. A few questions will help us to do this.

1. When did God begin to love us?

2. Why does He love us?

3. How or in what way does He love us?

4. How much does He love us?

5. How can we know that He loves us?

6. What can we give back to Him for His love?

We will consider these questions one by one.

WHEN DID GOD BEGIN TO LOVE US?

The LORD has appeared of old to me, saying: "Yes, I have loved you with an everlasting love; therefore with lovingkindness I have drawn you."

JEREMIAH 31:3

He chose us in Him before the foundation of the world, that we should be holy and without blame before Him in love, having predestined us to adoption as sons by Jesus Christ to Himself, according to the good pleasure of His will.   EPHESIANS 1:4–5

God has always been love, and therefore He has always loved us. His love has no beginning because it is from everlasting; and it has no ending because it is to everlasting.

Who shall separate us from the love of Christ? Shall tribulation, or distress, or persecution, or famine, or nakedness, or peril, or sword?...For I am persuaded that neither death nor life, nor angels nor principalities nor powers, nor things present nor things to come, nor height nor depth, nor any other created thing, shall be able to separate us from the love of God which is in Christ Jesus our Lord.   ROMANS 8:35, 38–39

Some people think that God loves us because we love Him, and that He does not begin to love us until we first love Him. But in the nature of things, the truth must be exactly the other way around.

In this is love, not that we loved God, but that He loved us and sent His Son to be the propitiation for our sins....We love Him because He first loved us.
                                    1 JOHN 4:10, 19

Our great need, therefore, is to find out that He loves us. Our question to one another or to our own hearts should not be, "Do you love God?" but "Do you know that God loves you?"

WHY DOES GOD LOVE US?

Beloved, let us love one another, for love is of God; and everyone who loves is born of God and knows God. He who does not love does not know God, for God is love.   1 JOHN 4:7–8

God loves us because He is love and cannot help loving. It is His nature to love, just as the sun is light and cannot help shining because it is its nature to shine.

The LORD did not set His love on you nor choose you because you were more in number than any

other people, for you were the least of all peoples; but because the LORD loves you, and because He would keep the oath which He swore to your fathers, the LORD has brought you out with a mighty hand, and redeemed you from the house of bondage, from the hand of Pharaoh king of Egypt.
                                       DEUTERONOMY 7:7–8

He loves us simply because He has chosen to love us, because He created us and we belong to Him. A creator always loves the thing he creates.

But God demonstrates His own love toward us, in that while we were still sinners, Christ died for us.
                                       ROMANS 5:8

But God, who is rich in mercy, because of His great love with which He loved us, even when we were dead in trespasses, made us alive together with Christ (by grace you have been saved), and raised us up together, and made us sit together in the heavenly places in Christ Jesus, that in the ages to come He might show the exceeding riches of His grace in His kindness toward us in Christ Jesus.
                                       EPHESIANS 2:4–7

God does not wait for us to become good before He will love us. He loves us while we are still sinners. He hates our sin, but He loves us. In this respect, He is just like a mother.

Sometimes children are taught, "God will not love you if you are naughty." But this is slander against our God, who is love. No mother would permit such a thing to be said against herself—that she did not love her child when he was naughty. It is her very love for the little naughty child that strengthens her to punish him, in order that she may make him good.

And you have forgotten the exhortation which speaks to you as to sons: "My son, do not despise the chastening of the LORD, nor be discouraged when you are rebuked by Him; for whom the LORD loves He chastens, and scourges every son whom He receives." If you endure chastening, God deals with you as with sons; for what son is there whom a father does not chasten? But if you are without chastening, of which all have become partakers, then you are illegitimate and not sons. Furthermore, we have had human fathers who corrected us, and we paid them respect. Shall we not much more readily be in subjection to the Father of spirits and live? For they indeed for a few days chastened us as seemed best to them, but He for our profit, that we may be partakers of His holiness.   HEBREWS 12:5–10

Our sinfulness only brings out a fresh expression of God's love in the form of chastening. It is only those we love whom we care to see perfected.

HOW OR IN WHAT WAY DOES GOD LOVE US?

God Loves Us as a Creator

But now, thus says the LORD, who created you, O Jacob, and He who formed you, O Israel: "Fear not, for I have redeemed you; I have called you by your name; you are Mine. When you pass through the waters, I will be with you; and through the rivers, they shall not overflow you. When you walk through the fire, you shall not be burned, nor shall the flame scorch you." ISAIAH 43:1–2

I have formed you, you are My servant; O Israel, you will not be forgotten by Me! I have blotted out, like a thick cloud, your transgressions, and like a cloud, your sins. Return to Me, for I have redeemed you. ISAIAH 44:21–22

We all know how much we delight in anything we create. We like to show it to our friends, and to look at it ourselves. We are careful to keep it safe, and we defend it when anyone criticizes it. This joy of ours in creation and ownership will help us to understand and believe in the love of our Creator for us, for we are "the work of His hands" (Job 34:19).

God Loves Us as Our Redeemer

I will mention the lovingkindnesses of the LORD and the praises of the LORD, according to all that the LORD has bestowed on us, and the great goodness toward the house of Israel, which He has bestowed on them according to His mercies, according to the multitude of His lovingkindnesses. For He said, "Surely they are My people, children who will not lie." So He became their Savior. In all their affliction He was afflicted, and the Angel of His Presence saved them; in His love and in His pity He redeemed them; and He bore them and carried them all the days of old. ISAIAH 63:7–9

"For I, the LORD your God, will hold your right hand, saying to you, 'Fear not, I will help you.'

Fear not, you worm Jacob, you men of Israel! I will help you," says the LORD and your Redeemer, the Holy One of Israel.   ISAIAH 41:13–14

Into Your hand I commit my spirit; You have redeemed me, O LORD God of truth.   PSALM 31:5

Hear the word of the LORD, O nations, and declare it in the isles afar off, and say, "He who scattered Israel will gather him, and keep him as a shepherd does his flock." For the LORD has redeemed Jacob, and ransomed him from the hand of one stronger than he.   JEREMIAH 31:10–11

God Loves Us as a Father

He shall cry to Me, "You are my Father, my God, and the rock of my salvation."   PSALM 89:26

And His name will be called...Everlasting Father.
                                   ISAIAH 9:6

They shall come with weeping, and with supplications I will lead them. I will cause them to walk by the rivers of waters, in a straight way in which they shall not stumble; for I am a Father to Israel, and Ephraim is My firstborn.   JEREMIAH 31:9

As a father pities his children, so the LORD pities those who fear Him.   PSALM 103:13

And he [the Prodigal Son] arose and came to his father. But when he was still a great way off, his father saw him and had compassion, and ran and fell on his neck and kissed him. And the son said to him, "Father, I have sinned against heaven and in your sight, and am no longer worthy to be called your son." But the father said to his servants, "Bring out the best robe and put it on him, and put a ring on his hand and sandals on his feet. And bring the fatted calf here and kill it, and let us eat and be merry; for this my son was dead and is alive again; he was lost and is found." And they began to be merry.   LUKE 15:20–24

When our Lord gave this divine picture of what a father is in the above passage, it was in reply to the Pharisees and scribes, who had murmured, saying, "This Man receives sinners and eats with them" (Luke 15:2). In Jesus' reply, He silenced forever every unbelieving thought that could make God out to be less tender than the human fathers He has made.

God Loves Us as a Mother

As one whom his mother comforts, so I will comfort you; and you shall be comforted in Jerusalem.
                                                 ISAIAH 66:13

Sing, O heavens! Be joyful, O earth! And break out in singing, O mountains! For the LORD has comforted His people, and will have mercy on His afflicted. But Zion said, "The LORD has forsaken me, and my Lord has forgotten me." "Can a woman forget her nursing child, and not have compassion on the son of her womb? Surely they may forget, yet I will not forget you. See, I have inscribed you on the palms of My hands; your walls are continually before Me."   ISAIAH 49:13–16

God Loves Us as a Friend

[Jesus said,] "Greater love has no one than this, than to lay down one's life for his friends. You are My friends if you do whatever I command you. No longer do I call you servants, for a servant does not know what his master is doing; but I have called you friends, for all things that I heard from My Father I have made known to you."   JOHN 15:13–15

So the LORD spoke to Moses face to face, as a man speaks to his friend.   EXODUS 33:11

But you, Israel, are My servant, Jacob whom I have chosen, the descendants of Abraham My friend.   ISAIAH 41:8

And the Scripture was fulfilled which says, "Abraham believed God, and it was accounted to him for righteousness." And he was called the friend of God.   JAMES 2:23

A man who has friends must himself be friendly, but there is a friend who sticks closer than a brother.   PROVERBS 18:24

Everything that our highest ideal of friendship implies must be ours in a friendship with God.

God Loves Us as a Brother

For whom He foreknew, He also predestined to be conformed to the image of His Son, that He might be the firstborn among many brethren.
ROMANS 8:29

34

For both He who sanctifies and those who are being sanctified are all of one, for which reason He is not ashamed to call them brethren, saying: "I will declare Your name to My brethren; in the midst of the assembly I will sing praise to You." And again: "I will put My trust in Him." And again: "Here am I and the children whom God has given Me." Inasmuch then as the children have partaken of flesh and blood, He Himself likewise shared in the same, that through death He might destroy him who had the power of death, that is, the devil, and release those who through fear of death were all their lifetime subject to bondage. For indeed He does not give aid to angels, but He does give aid to the seed of Abraham. Therefore, in all things He had to be made like His brethren, that He might be a merciful and faithful High Priest in things pertaining to God, to make propitiation for the sins of the people. For in that He Himself has suffered, being tempted, He is able to aid those who are tempted.   HEBREWS 2:11–18

The next three passages contain the divine declaration of what brotherly love is.

Finally, all of you be of one mind, having compassion for one another; love as brothers, be tenderhearted, be courteous; not returning evil for evil or reviling for reviling, but on the contrary blessing, knowing that you were called to this, that you may inherit a blessing.   1 PETER 3:8–9

If a brother or sister is naked and destitute of daily food, and one of you says to them, "Depart in peace, be warmed and filled," but you do not give them the things which are needed for the body, what does it profit?   JAMES 2:15–16

By this we know love, because He laid down His life for us. And we also ought to lay down our lives for the brethren. But whoever has this world's goods, and sees his brother in need, and shuts up his heart from him, how does the love of God abide in him?   1 JOHN 3:16–17

What God tells us we ought to be as brethren, that He surely must be Himself. In His brotherhood, therefore, we find an assurance of His infinite love and care.

God Loves Us as a Shepherd

Know that the LORD, He is God; it is He who has made us, and not we ourselves; we are His people and the sheep of His pasture.   PSALM 100:3

For He is our God, and we are the people of His pasture, and the sheep of His hand.   PSALM 95:7

The LORD is my shepherd; I shall not want. He makes me to lie down in green pastures; He leads me beside the still waters.   PSALM 23:1–2

[Jesus said,] "I am the good shepherd. The good shepherd gives His life for the sheep....The hireling flees because he is a hireling and does not care about the sheep. I am the good shepherd; and I know My sheep, and am known by My own."
                              JOHN 10:11, 13–14

He will feed His flock like a shepherd; He will gather the lambs with His arm, and carry them in His bosom, and gently lead those who are with young.   ISAIAH 40:11

God Loves Us as a Bridegroom

You shall no longer be termed Forsaken, nor shall your land any more be termed Desolate; but you shall be called Hephzibah [My Delight Is in Her], and your land Beulah [Married]; for the LORD delights in you, and your land shall be married. For... as the bridegroom rejoices over the bride, so shall your God rejoice over you.   ISAIAH 62:4–5

[John the Baptist said concerning Jesus,] "He who has the bride is the bridegroom; but the friend of the bridegroom, who stands and hears him, rejoices greatly because of the bridegroom's voice. Therefore this joy of mine is fulfilled."   JOHN 3:29

Then the disciples of John came to Him, saying, "Why do we and the Pharisees fast often, but Your disciples do not fast?" And Jesus said to them, "Can the friends of the bridegroom mourn as long as the bridegroom is with them? But the days will come when the bridegroom will be taken away from them, and then they will fast."
                              MATTHEW 9:14–15

Therefore, my brethren, you also have become dead to the law through the body of Christ, that you may be married to another; to Him who was raised from the dead, that we should bear fruit to God.   ROMANS 7:4

Then one of the seven angels who had the seven bowls filled with the seven last plagues came to me and talked with me, saying, "Come, I will show you the bride, the Lamb's wife."

REVELATION 21:9

No words are needed to tell us of a bridegroom's joy over his bride, yet it is only a faint picture of God's joy over us!

God Loves Us As He Loves Himself

Husbands, love your wives, just as Christ also loved the church and gave Himself for her, that He might sanctify and cleanse her with the washing of water by the word, that He might present her to Himself a glorious church, not having spot or wrinkle or any such thing, but that she should be holy and without blemish. So husbands ought to love their own wives as their own bodies; he who loves his wife loves himself. For no one ever hated his own flesh, but nourishes and cherishes it, just as the Lord does the church. For we are members of His body, of His flesh and of His bones. "For this reason a man shall leave his father and mother and be joined to his wife, and the two shall become one flesh." This is a great mystery, but I speak concerning Christ and the church.

EPHESIANS 5:25–32

HOW MUCH DOES GOD LOVE US?

May [you] be able to comprehend with all the saints what is the width and length and depth and height; to know the love of Christ which passes knowledge; that you may be filled with all the fullness of God.   EPHESIANS 3:18–19

Notice that it is a love that "passes knowledge." All we know or can imagine of earthly love cannot make us understand the height, the depth, the length, and the width of this infinite, everlasting, unchangeable, divine love.

[Jesus said,] "I have declared to them Your name, and will declare it, that the love with which You loved Me may be in them, and I in them."
                                                              JOHN 17:26

[Jesus said,] "The glory which You gave Me I have given them, that they may be one just as We are one: I in them, and You in Me; that they may be made perfect in one, and that the world may know that You have sent Me, and have loved them as You have loved Me."   JOHN 17:22–23

[Jesus said,] "As the Father loved Me, I also have loved you; abide in My love."   JOHN 15:9

Notice the words *as* and *also* in the above passage. Believe the wondrous fact they express, even though you may not be able to comprehend it. As the hymn says,

> How Thou canst think so well of us,
>   And be the God Thou art,
> Is darkness to my intellect,
>   But sunshine to my heart.

Read the divine description of love in 1 Corinthians 13:1–13, and apply each word of it to Christ as showing what sort of love He has.

HOW CAN WE KNOW THAT GOD LOVES US?

[Jesus said,] "For God so loved the world that He gave His only begotten Son, that whoever believes in Him should not perish but have everlasting life. For God did not send His Son into the world to condemn the world, but that the world through Him might be saved."   JOHN 3:16–17

By this we know ["perceive" KJV] love, because He laid down His life for us. And we also ought to lay down our lives for the brethren.
1 JOHN 3:16

In this the love of God was manifested toward us, that God has sent His only begotten Son into the world, that we might live through Him.   1 JOHN 4:9

God's love was not *caused* by the work of Christ; it was simply "manifested." All we can do is "perceive" it. In spiritual things, we perceive by believing. Our friends may love us and may tell us so a thousand times and give us continual proofs of love. But unless we believe in their love, we will never really perceive it or possess it. Faith is necessary for the possession of human love, and faith is equally necessary for the possession of divine love. God gives us His love always, but we cannot perceive and possess it unless we believe in it.

WHAT CAN WE GIVE BACK TO GOD FOR HIS LOVE?

We can place our faith in it.

What shall I render to the LORD for all His benefits toward me? I will take up the cup of salvation, and call upon the name of the LORD. I will pay my vows to the LORD now in the presence of all His people.   PSALM 116:12–14

How precious is Your lovingkindness, O God! Therefore the children of men put their trust under the shadow of Your wings.   PSALM 36:7

And we have known and believed the love that God has for us.   1 JOHN 4:16

The first response to love is to believe in it and accept its goodness. Nothing grieves love so much as a lack of trust on the part of the beloved one. You wound the Lord more by your doubts of His love than by all your other sins put together. If a naughty child were to entertain doubts of his mother's love, this would be the hardest of all to bear. Let our utmost confidence, then, be our first reaction to this wondrous love of God.

We love Him because He first loved us.
                        1 JOHN 4:19

When we know and believe in God's love, it will draw out ours in return. God *wins* our love. Just as a bridegroom wins the love of his bride by assurances and proofs of his love for her, so our God win ours. "We love Him because He first loved us." Obedience will then follow.

> This is love, that we walk according to His commandments.
> 2 JOHN 6

> For this is the love of God, that we keep His commandments. And His commandments are not burdensome.
> 1 JOHN 5:3

> Jesus answered and said to him, "If anyone loves Me, he will keep My word; and My Father will love him, and We will come to him and make Our home with him. He who does not love Me does not keep My words; and the word which you hear is not Mine but the Father's who sent Me."
> JOHN 14:23–24

Love is not talk but action. If we love, we will obey. Obedience is always the test of love. It is easy to talk about our love for God, and even to work ourselves up into an emotion of love. But unless our love stands the test of "walk[ing] according to His commandments" (2 John 6), it is nothing but an unreal sentiment.

> Love has been perfected among us in this: that we may have boldness in the day of judgment; because as He is, so are we in this world. There is no fear in love; but perfect love casts out fear, because fear involves torment. But he who fears has not been made perfect in love.
> 1 JOHN 4:17–18

Let us ask ourselves the searching question as to whether all fear that involves torment has been cast out of our hearts. Have we so "known and believed the love that God has for us" (1 John 4:16) that we have been delivered from all fear, care, and anxiety? Have our hearts been kept in perfect peace because we have trusted in Him (Isaiah 26:3)?

God Is Love

Like a cradle, rocking, rocking,
   Silent, peaceful, to and fro;
Like a mother's sweet looks dropping
   On the little face below;
Hangs the green earth, swinging, turning,
   Jarless, noiseless, safe and slow;
Falls the light of God's face bending
   Down, and watching us below.

And as feeble babes that suffer,
   Toss and cry, and will not rest,
Are the ones the tender mother
   Holds the closest, loves the best;
So when we are weak and wretched,
   By our sins weighed down, distressed,
Then it is that God's great patience
   Holds us closest, loves us best.

Oh, great heart of God, whose loving
   Cannot hindered be, nor crossed;
Will not weary, will not even
   In our death itself be lost!
Love divine! Of such great loving
   Only mothers know the cost,
Cost of love, that, all love passing,
   Gave itself to save the lost!

Chapter 3

The Law and the Gospel

For if that first covenant had been faultless, then no place would have been sought for a second. Because finding fault with them, He says: "Behold, the days are coming, says the LORD, when I will make a new covenant with the house of Israel and with the house of Judah; not according to the covenant that I made with their fathers in the day when I took them by the hand to lead them out of the land of Egypt; because they did not continue in My covenant, and I disregarded them, says the LORD. For this is the covenant that I will make with the house of Israel after those days, says the LORD: I will put My laws in their mind and write them on their hearts; and I will be their God, and they shall be My people. None of them shall teach his neighbor, and none his brother, saying, 'Know the LORD,' for all shall know Me, from the least of them to the greatest of them. For I will be merciful to their unrighteousness, and their sins and their lawless deeds I will remember no more." In that He

says, "A new covenant," He has made the first obsolete.
Now what is becoming obsolete and growing old
is ready to vanish away.
—Hebrews 8:7–13

The old covenant, which is here declared to have been put away in order to make room for "a new covenant," is the covenant of an outward law. In the nature of things, the old covenant of an outward law grows old and vanishes with the coming of the new covenant of an inward life. That is, as long as a man is a thief at heart, he needs an outward law to keep him from stealing; but as soon as he becomes honest at heart, he no longer needs the outward law.

But if you are led by the Spirit, you are not under the law....But the fruit of the Spirit is love, joy, peace, longsuffering, kindness, goodness, faithfulness, gentleness, self-control. Against such there is no law.   GALATIANS 5:18, 22–23

The old covenant is based on the principle of work and wages—so much work results in so much wages, no more, no less.

The new covenant, on the contrary, is based on the principle of life and fruit. "We love Him because He first loved us" (1 John 4:19), and *therefore* we serve Him. He has bestowed upon us a new life from Himself, and the fulfilling of the law is simply the *fruit* of the new life thus given.

I will put My Spirit within you and cause you to walk in My statutes, and you will keep My judgments and do them.   EZEKIEL 36:27

Christ is called "the Mediator of the new covenant" (Hebrews 9:15), and the covenant is called the new testament of our Lord and Savior Jesus Christ. This, therefore, is the covenant under which we live, even "the power of an endless life," as the following passage tells us.

In the likeness of Melchizedek, there arises another priest who has come, not according to the law of a fleshly commandment, but according to the power of an endless life. For He testifies: "You are a priest forever according to the order of Melchizedek." For on the one hand there is an annulling of the former commandment because of its weakness and unprofitableness, for the law made nothing perfect; on the other hand, there is the bringing in of a better hope, through which we draw near to God.   HEBREWS 7:15–19

The following contrasts will show the difference between the old covenant and the new.

The law says, *Do, and then you will live.*

The Gospel says, *Live, and then you will do.*

The Law	The Gospel
For Moses writes about the righteousness which is of the law, "The man who does those things shall live by them." (ROMANS 10:5)	For the law of the Spirit of life in Christ Jesus has made me free from the law of sin and death. For what the law could not do in that it was weak through

Yet the law is not of faith, but "the man who does them shall live by them." (GALATIANS 3:12)

the flesh, God did by sending His own Son in the likeness of sinful flesh, on account of sin: He condemned sin in the flesh, that the righteous requirement of the law might be fulfilled in us who do not walk according to the flesh but according to the Spirit. (ROMANS 8:2–4)

The law says, *Pay what you owe!*

The Gospel says, *I freely forgive all.*

The Law

If a man causes disfigurement of his neighbor, as he has done, so shall it be done to him; fracture for fracture, eye for eye, tooth for tooth; as he has caused disfigurement of a man, so shall it be done to him. (LEVITICUS 24:19–20)

Your eye shall not pity: life shall be for life, eye for eye, tooth for tooth, hand for hand, foot for foot. (DEUTERONOMY 19:21)

You have heard that it was said, "An eye for an

The Gospel

And Jesus answered and said to him, "Simon, I have something to say to you." So he said, "Teacher, say it." "There was a certain creditor who had two debtors. One owed five hundred denarii, and the other fifty. And when they had nothing with which to repay, he freely forgave them both. Tell Me, therefore, which of them will love him more?" Simon answered and said, "I suppose the one whom he forgave more." And He

47

eye and a tooth for a tooth." (MATTHEW 5:38)

But that servant went out and found one of his fellow servants who owed him a hundred denarii; and he laid hands on him and took him by the throat, saying, "Pay me what you owe!" (MATTHEW 18:28)

said to him, "You have rightly judged." (LUKE 7:40–43)

Then Jesus said, "Father, forgive them, for they do not know what they do." (LUKE 23:34)

Therefore let it be known to you, brethren, that through this Man is preached to you the forgiveness of sins; and by Him everyone who believes is justified from all things from which you could not be justified by the law of Moses. (ACTS 13:38–39)

The law says, *"Get yourselves a new heart and a new spirit."*

The spirit of the Gospel says, *"I will give you a new heart and put a new spirit within you."*

The Law

Cast away from you all the transgressions which you have committed, and get yourselves a new heart and a new spirit. For why

The Gospel

Then I will sprinkle clean water on you, and you shall be clean; I will cleanse you from all your filthiness and from all should you die, O house of Israel? (EZEKIEL 18:31) your idols. I will give you a new heart and put a new spirit within you; I will take the heart of stone out of your flesh and give you a heart of flesh. (EZEKIEL 36:25–26)

The law says, *Love God.*

The Gospel says, *God loves you.*

The Law	The Gospel
You shall love the LORD your God with all your heart, with all your soul, and with all your strength. (DEUTERONOMY 6:5)	In this is love, not that we loved God, but that He loved us and sent His Son to be the propitiation for our sins....We love Him because He first loved us. (1 JOHN 4:10, 19)

The law pronounces curses.

The Gospel announces blessings.

The Law	The Gospel
For as many as are of the works of the law are under the curse; for it is written, "Cursed is everyone who does not continue in all things which are written in	Just as David also describes the blessedness of the man to whom God imputes righteousness apart from works: "Blessed are those whose lawless deeds

the book of the law, to do them." (GALATIANS 3:10)

are forgiven, and whose sins are covered; blessed is the man to whom the LORD shall not impute sin." (ROMANS 4:6–8)

The law deals with wages.

The Gospel bestows gifts.

The Law

For the wages of sin is death. (ROMANS 6:23)

Now to him who works, the wages are not counted as grace but as debt. (ROMANS 4:4)

The Gospel

The gift of God is eternal life in Christ Jesus our Lord. (ROMANS 6:23)

But to him who does not work but believes on Him who justifies the ungodly, his faith is accounted for righteousness. (ROMANS 4:5)

The law demands holiness.

The Gospel gives holiness.

The Law

Speak to all the congregation of the children of Israel, and say to them: "You shall be holy, for I the LORD your God am holy." (LEVITICUS 19:2)

The Gospel

For sin shall not have dominion over you, for you are not under law but under grace....But now having been set free from sin, and having become slaves

And the LORD commanded us to observe all these statutes, to fear the LORD our God, for our good always, that He might preserve us alive, as it is this day. Then it will be righteousness for us, if we are careful to observe all these commandments before the LORD our God, as He has commanded us. (DEUTERONOMY 6:24–25)

of God, you have your fruit to holiness, and the end, everlasting life. (ROMANS 6:14, 22)

For by grace you have been saved through faith, and that not of yourselves; it is the gift of God, not of works, lest anyone should boast. For we are His workmanship, created in Christ Jesus for good works, which God prepared beforehand that we should walk in them. (EPHESIANS 2:8–10)

The law says, *Do.*

The Gospel says, *Done.*

The Law

The Gospel

Therefore you shall keep the commandment, the statutes, and the judgments which I command you today, to observe them. Then it shall come to pass, because you listen to these judgments, and keep and do them, that the LORD your God will keep with you the covenant and the

[Jesus said,] "I have glorified You on the earth. I have finished the work which You have given Me to do." (JOHN 17:4)

Blessed be the God and Father of our Lord Jesus Christ, who has blessed us with every spiritual blessing in the heavenly places mercy which He swore to your fathers. (DEUTERO-NOMY 7:11–12)

in Christ....In Him we have redemption through His blood, the forgiveness of sins, according to the riches of His grace. (EPHE-SIANS 1:3, 7)

The law extorts the unwilling service of a slave.

The Gospel wins the loving service of a son.

The Law

Or do you not know, brethren (for I speak to those who know the law), that the law has dominion over a man as long as he lives? For the woman who has a husband is bound by the law to her husband as long as he lives. But if the husband dies, she is released from the law of her husband. (ROMANS 7:1–2)

But before faith came, we were kept under guard by the law, kept for the faith which would afterward be revealed. Therefore the law was our tutor to bring us to Christ, that we might be

The Gospel

But after faith has come, we are no longer under a tutor. For you are all sons of God through faith in Christ Jesus. (GALATIANS 3:25–26)

But now we have been delivered from the law, having died to what we were held by, so that we should serve in the newness of the Spirit and not in the oldness of the let-ter. (ROMANS 7:6)

Stand fast therefore in the liberty by which Christ has made us free, and do not be entangled again with a

justified by faith. (GALA-
TIANS 3:23–24)

yoke of bondage. (GALA-
TIANS 5:1)

The law makes blessings the result of obedience.

The Gospel makes obedience the result of blessings.

The Law	The Gospel
Now it shall come to pass, if you diligently obey the voice of the LORD your God, to observe carefully all His commandments which I command you today, that the LORD your God will set you high above all nations of the earth. And all these blessings shall come upon you and overtake you, because you obey the voice of the LORD your God. (DEUTERONOMY 28:1–2)	Behold what manner of love the Father has bestowed on us, that we should be called children of God! Therefore the world does not know us, because it did not know Him. Beloved, now we are children of God; and it has not yet been revealed what we shall be, but we know that when He is revealed, we shall be like Him, for we shall see Him as He is. And everyone who has this hope in Him purifies himself, just as He is pure. (1 JOHN 3:1–3)

The law says *if*.

The Gospel says *therefore*.

The Law

The LORD will establish you as a holy people to Himself, just as He has sworn to you, if you keep the commandments of the LORD your God and walk in His ways....But it shall come to pass, if you do not obey the voice of the LORD your God, to observe carefully all His commandments and His statutes which I command you today, that all these curses will come upon you and overtake you. (DEUTERONOMY 28:9, 15)

The Gospel

Therefore, having these promises, beloved, let us cleanse ourselves from all filthiness of the flesh and spirit, perfecting holiness in the fear of God. (2 CORINTHIANS 7:1)

I beseech you therefore, brethren, by the mercies of God, that you present your bodies a living sacrifice, holy, acceptable to God, which is your reasonable service. (ROMANS 12:1)

Under the law, God's dealings with man were to show him his own helplessness.

Under the Gospel, God's dealings with man are to show him the mighty power of his Savior.

The Law

Moreover the law entered that the offense might abound. But where sin abounded, grace abounded much more. (ROMANS 5:20)

The Gospel

And lest I should be exalted above measure by the abundance of the revelations, a thorn in the flesh was given to me, a messenger of Satan to

What shall we say then? Is the law sin? Certainly not! On the contrary, I would not have known sin except through the law. For I would not have known covetousness unless the law had said, "You shall not covet." But sin, taking opportunity by the commandment, produced in me all manner of evil desire. For apart from the law sin was dead. I was alive once without the law, but when the commandment came, sin revived and I died. And the commandment, which was to bring life, I found to bring death. For sin, taking occasion by the commandment, deceived me, and by it killed me. Therefore the law is holy, and the commandment holy and just and good. Has then what is good become death to me? Certainly not! But sin, that it might appear sin, was producing death in me through what is good, so that sin through the commandment might buffet me, lest I be exalted above measure. Concerning this thing I pleaded with the Lord three times that it might depart from me. And He said to me, "My grace is sufficient for you, for My strength is made perfect in weakness." Therefore most gladly I will rather boast in my infirmities, that the power of Christ may rest upon me. Therefore I take pleasure in infirmities, in reproaches, in needs, in persecutions, in distresses, for Christ's sake. For when I am weak, then I am strong. (2 CORINTHIANS 12:7–10)

become exceedingly sinful.
(ROMANS 7:7–13)

The law places the day of rest at the end of the week's work.

The Gospel places the day of rest at the beginning of the week's work.

The law was given to restrain the "old man" (Ephesians 4:22).

The Gospel was given to bestow liberty upon the "new man" (Ephesians 4:24).

The law was given to put to death.

The Gospel was given to make alive.

The epistle to the Galatians deals with this subject more fully than any other part of Scripture. The Galatians did not seem to understand the vital difference between the two covenants and were trying to mix them together. They did not deny Christ and the new life in Him, but they tried to add something to Christ, thus trying to enslave the new life to the law that was made for the old life. Christ *and* the law was the heresy that caused Paul to cry out, "O foolish Galatians! Who has bewitched you?" (Galatians 3:1). Their idea was Christ *and* legal observances.

The Galatians seem to have begun all right, for Paul said they had received the Spirit "by the hearing of faith" (verse 2). They had been taught at first that the Lord Jesus Christ is a complete Savior, and they seem to have trusted Him as such. But some Jewish brethren had come among them and said, "Oh no, you are very much mistaken; Christ alone is not enough. You must come under the Jewish law as well." They *added* external rites to the work of Christ.

We in the present day are shocked at this, but in principle many people do the same thing today. They do not add Jewish ceremonies, but they add some other form of legality—some self-effort of one kind or another. It does not make much difference what we add; the wrong thing is to add anything at all as being *necessary* to salvation. Many things may be necessary as the fruits or results of salvation, but as the procuring cause and the inward power, only the redemption that is in Christ, and the life hidden with Him in God, can avail whatsoever.

The religion of the law is like making an apple orchard by first buying some apples and tying them onto branches, then fastening the branches onto the trunk, and then fastening the trunk onto the roots, and then finally getting a field and planting these manufactured trees. First the fruit, afterward the roots. But the religion of the Gospel begins at the roots, then grows up and blooms into flowers and fruit, which are "love, joy, peace" (Galatians 5:22).

O foolish Galatians! Who has bewitched you that you should not obey the truth, before whose eyes Jesus Christ was clearly portrayed among you as crucified? This only I want to learn from you: Did you receive the Spirit by the works of the law, or by the hearing of faith? Are you so foolish? Having begun in the Spirit, are you now being made perfect by the flesh? Have you suffered so many things in vain; if indeed it was in vain?...But that no one is justified by the law in the sight of God is evident, for "the just shall live by faith." Yet the law is not of faith, but "the man who does them shall live by them."   GALATIANS 3:1–4, 11–12

Is the law then against the promises of God? Certainly not! For if there had been a law given which could have given life, truly righteousness would have been by the law. But the Scripture has confined all under sin, that the promise by faith in Jesus Christ might be given to those who believe. But before faith came, we were kept under guard by the law, kept for the faith which would afterward be revealed.   GALATIANS 3:21–23

Now I say that the heir, as long as he is a child, does not differ at all from a slave, though he is master of all, but is under guardians and stewards until the time appointed by the father. Even so we, when we were children, were in bondage under the elements of the world. But when the fullness of the time had come, God sent forth His Son, born of a woman, born under the law, to redeem those who were under the law, that we might receive the adoption as sons. And because you are sons, God has sent forth the Spirit of His Son into your hearts, crying out, "Abba, Father!" Therefore you are no longer a slave but a son, and if a son, then an heir of God through Christ. But then, indeed, when you did not know God, you served those which by nature are not gods. But now after you have known God, or rather are known by God, how is it that you turn again to the weak and beggarly elements, to which you desire again to be in bondage? You observe days and months and seasons and years. I am afraid for you, lest I have labored for you in vain.   GALATIANS 4:1–11

Finally, Paul summed up the whole subject in an emphatic exhortation, which applies to us now no less than it did to the Galatians then.

Stand fast therefore in the liberty by which Christ has made us free, and do not be entangled again with a yoke of bondage....You have become estranged from Christ, you who attempt to be justified by law; you have fallen from grace. For we through the Spirit eagerly wait for the hope of righteousness by faith. For in Christ Jesus neither circumcision nor uncircumcision avails anything, but faith working through love.

GALATIANS 5:1, 4–6

In the following significant words, Paul announced the inward secret of the new and victorious life, which needs no law, because it is a law unto itself in its very depths:

I say then: Walk in the Spirit, and you shall not fulfill the lust of the flesh....But if you are led by the Spirit, you are not under the law....And those who are Christ's have crucified the flesh with its passions and desires. If we live in the Spirit, let us also walk in the Spirit.   GALATIANS 5:16, 18, 24–25

"Against such there is no law" (Galatians 5:23) is the divine declaration concerning all who thus live and walk in the Spirit.

Only those who inwardly desire to break the law are in any sense "under the law" (verse 18). The person who approves of the law and intends to keep it is over it, not under it. The law is a terror to evildoers only, not to those who do good (Romans 13:3). Some of us walk through the streets of our great cities without a thought of the policemen, except as our protectors and friends, while others shrink from them as their bitterest enemies.

Therefore, let us seek to lay aside all the old legal life of self-effort and self-dependence. Let us open our hearts wide to allow the overcoming life of Christ to take full possession of us, and to work in us to will and to do all the good pleasure of God (Philippians 2:13).

For whatever is born of God overcomes the world. And this is the victory that has overcome the world; our faith. Who is he who overcomes the world, but he who believes that Jesus is the Son of God?   1 JOHN 5:4–5

Chapter 4

Assurance of Salvation

*Let us draw near with a true heart in full assurance of
faith, having our hearts sprinkled from an evil conscience
and our bodies washed with pure water.*
—Hebrews 10:22

By the "assurance of faith" is meant the assurance of salvation—in other words, a clear and
definite knowledge of the forgiveness of sins, of reconciliation with God, and of having God as our Father.

About these vital matters we must be able to
say, "I know." Not "I hope so" or "I wish so," but
firmly and unhesitatingly, "I know."

Blessed are the people who know the joyful sound!
They walk, O LORD, in the light of Your countenance. In Your name they rejoice all day long, and
in Your righteousness they are exalted.

PSALM 89:15–16

You shall know that I, the LORD, am your Savior
and your Redeemer, the Mighty One of Jacob.

ISAIAH 60:16

61

[Jesus said,] "At that day you will know that I am in My Father, and you in Me, and I in you."

JOHN 14:20

IS IT NORMAL FOR A CHRISTIAN TO DOUBT HIS SALVATION?

This assurance is necessary for all right living. It ought to be the first step in the Christian life. In the absence of this assurance lies the cause of much of the failure of Christians. An uncertain Christian presents the anomaly of a child who doubts his parentage, of an heir who is afraid to take possession of his inheritance, of a bride who is not sure she has really been married.

What could we expect from such doubts in earthly relationships but indifference, fear, anxiety, unkindness, sorrow, and rebellion? Are these not the very things that are found far too often in the hearts of God's children, in reference to their relationship to Him?

You did not serve the LORD your God with joy and gladness of heart.   DEUTERONOMY 28:47–48

No soul can serve the Lord with joyfulness when it is in doubt about the reality or the stability of its relationship with Him. Concerning earthly relationships, all human comfort is destroyed in such a state of doubt and instability. We all know that, in the same way, little divine comfort is to be found in a doubtful spiritual relationship.

Can we suppose for a moment that this too frequent reign of doubt in Christians' hearts is God's plan for His people? Does the Bible teach that it is?

I answer most emphatically, No! A thousand times, No!

The Old Testament nowhere portrays the Israelites as not knowing whether they were Israelites or not. Every law given to them or promise made to them was founded on a previously acknowledged and understood fact—that they did indeed belong to the family of Israel and were in truth the people of God. Before they were allowed to join the Lord's army and fight His battles, they had to recite their ancestry.

[God said to Moses,] "Take a census of all the congregation of the children of Israel, by their families, by their fathers' houses, according to the number of names, every male individually, from twenty years old and above; all who are able to go to war in Israel. You and Aaron shall number them by their armies. And with you there shall be a man from every tribe, each one the head of his father's house."...And they assembled all the congregation together on the first day of the second month; and they recited their ancestry by families, by their fathers' houses, according to the number of names, from twenty years old and above, each one individually.   NUMBERS 1:2–4, 18

Furthermore, before they could enter into the office of priest, they had to find "their listing" and register "by genealogy," for no strangers were allowed to come near.

These sought their listing among those who were registered by genealogy, but they were not found; therefore they were excluded from the priesthood

as defiled. And the governor said to them that they
should not eat of the most holy things till a priest
could consult with the Urim and Thummim.

EZRA 2:62–63

So you shall appoint Aaron and his sons, and they
shall attend to their priesthood; but the outsider
who comes near shall be put to death.

NUMBERS 3:10

Similarly, we who are now God's people cannot
fight His battles effectively or enjoy true priestly
communion with Him until we also can recite our
ancestry (that we are the children of God) and register our genealogy (that we are born of Him).

And because you are sons, God has sent forth the
Spirit of His Son into your hearts, crying out,
"Abba, Father!" Therefore you are no longer a
slave but a son, and if a son, then an heir of God
through Christ.　　　　　　　　　GALATIANS 4:6–7

Behold what manner of love the Father has bestowed on us, that we should be called children of
God! Therefore the world does not know us, because it did not know Him. Beloved, now we are
children of God; and it has not yet been revealed
what we shall be, but we know that when He is revealed, we shall be like Him, for we shall see Him
as He is.　　　　　　　　　　　　　1 JOHN 3:1–2

We cannot have the attitude of a son until we
know that we are sons. To doubt our sonship would
be to lose the right attitude at once.

For as many as are led by the Spirit of God, these are sons of God. For you did not receive the spirit of bondage again to fear, but you received the Spirit of adoption by whom we cry out, "Abba, Father." The Spirit Himself bears witness with our spirit that we are children of God, and if children, then heirs; heirs of God and joint heirs with Christ, if indeed we suffer with Him, that we may also be glorified together.   ROMANS 8:14–17

BLESSED ASSURANCE IN THE NEW TESTAMENT

In the Gospels

Our Lord Himself always spoke to His disciples in terms of absolute certainty as to their relationship to God, as we see in the following verses:

Do not fear, little flock, for it is your Father's good pleasure to give you the kingdom.   LUKE 12:32

Nevertheless do not rejoice in this, that the spirits are subject to you, but rather rejoice because your names are written in heaven.   LUKE 10:20

And the glory which You gave Me I have given them, that they may be one just as We are one: I in them, and You in Me; that they may be made perfect in one, and that the world may know that You have sent Me, and have loved them as You have loved Me.   JOHN 17:22–23

Let not your heart be troubled; you believe in God, believe also in Me. In My Father's house are many mansions; if it were not so, I would have told you. I

go to prepare a place for you. And if I go and prepare a place for you, I will come again and receive
you to Myself; that where I am, there you may be
also.   JOHN 14:1–3

Jesus said, "If it were not so, I would have told
you." Surely we may trust Him and accept His
statements as facts, without any further questioning.

In the Book of Acts

Nowhere in the book of Acts do we find the
apostles, or any of the early believers, questioning
their standing or doubting their relationship with
the Lord. Concerning their experiences on the Day
of Pentecost, Peter said,

But this is what was spoken by the prophet Joel:
"And it shall come to pass in the last days, says
God, that I will pour out of My Spirit on all flesh;
your sons and your daughters shall prophesy, your
young men shall see visions, your old men shall
dream dreams. And on My menservants and on
My maidservants I will pour out My Spirit in those
days; and they shall prophesy."   ACTS 2:16–18

Elsewhere, Peter affirmed his certainty:

If we this day are judged for a good deed done to a
helpless man, by what means he has been made
well, let it be known to you all, and to all the people of Israel, that by the name of Jesus Christ of
Nazareth, whom you crucified, whom God raised

from the dead, by Him this man stands here before
you whole.   ACTS 4:9–10

For we cannot but speak the things which we have
seen and heard.   ACTS 4:20

No one can read the biblical accounts of the
words and deeds of the apostles and the early believers, without seeing that they were saturated through
and through with an utter certainty of their salvation in the Lord Jesus Christ. It was as much a part
of them as their nationality as Jews, or their birth in
Palestine, and was no more open to question.

Let us try to imagine them as being filled with
the doubts and questions of modern Christians, and
let us consider what effect such attitudes would have
had on their preaching and their work. We can see in
a moment that such a state would have been fatal to
the spread of the Gospel, and that a church founded
on doubts and questions could have made no head-
way in an unbelieving world.

In the Epistles

A tone of utter assurance runs throughout all
the Epistles. Every one of them is addressed to people of whom it was taken for granted that they knew
their standing as the reconciled and forgiven children of God, and the writers expressed the same assurance for themselves.

Paul, a bondservant of Jesus Christ, called to be
an apostle, separated to the gospel of God....To all
who are in Rome, beloved of God, called to be

saints: Grace to you and peace from God our Father and the Lord Jesus Christ.   ROMANS 1:1, 7

Paul, called to be an apostle of Jesus Christ through the will of God, and Sosthenes our brother, to the church of God which is at Corinth, to those who are sanctified in Christ Jesus, called to be saints, with all who in every place call on the name of Jesus Christ our Lord, both theirs and ours.
1 CORINTHIANS 1:1–2

Paul, Silvanus, and Timothy, to the church of the Thessalonians in God the Father and the Lord Jesus Christ: Grace to you and peace from God our Father and the Lord Jesus Christ. We give thanks to God always for you all, making mention of you in our prayers, remembering without ceasing your work of faith, labor of love, and patience of hope in our Lord Jesus Christ in the sight of our God and Father, knowing, beloved brethren, your election by God.   1 THESSALONIANS 1:1–4

Paul, a prisoner of Christ Jesus, and Timothy our brother, to Philemon our beloved friend and fellow laborer, to the beloved Apphia, Archippus our fellow soldier, and to the church in your house: Grace to you and peace from God our Father and the Lord Jesus Christ. I thank my God, making mention of you always in my prayers, hearing of your love and faith which you have toward the Lord Jesus and toward all the saints.   PHILEMON 1–5

Peter, an apostle of Jesus Christ, to the pilgrims of the Dispersion in Pontus, Galatia, Cappadocia, Asia, and Bithynia, elect according to the foreknowledge of God the Father, in sanctification of the Spirit, for obedience and sprinkling of the blood of Jesus Christ: Grace to you and peace be multiplied.

1 PETER 1:1–2

Simon Peter, a bondservant and apostle of Jesus Christ, to those who have obtained like precious faith with us by the righteousness of our God and Savior Jesus Christ.   2 PETER 1:1

That which was from the beginning, which we have heard, which we have seen with our eyes, which we have looked upon, and our hands have handled, concerning the Word of life; the life was manifested, and we have seen, and bear witness, and declare to you that eternal life which was with the Father and was manifested to us; that which we have seen and heard we declare to you, that you also may have fellowship with us; and truly our fellowship is with the Father and with His Son Jesus Christ.   1 JOHN 1:1–3

THE ELDER, to the elect lady and her children, whom I love in truth, and not only I, but also all those who have known the truth, because of the truth which abides in us and will be with us forever.   2 JOHN 1–2

Jude, a bondservant of Jesus Christ, and brother of James, to those who are called, sanctified by God the Father, and preserved in Jesus Christ.

JUDE 1

Again, if we look throughout the Epistles, we will invariably find that they, like the Gospels and the book of Acts, are saturated through and through with assurance. Nowhere is a doubt or a question of the believer's standing in the family of God even so much as hinted at or supposed possible.

Therefore, having been justified by faith, we have peace with God through our Lord Jesus Christ, through whom also we have access by faith into this grace in which we stand, and rejoice in hope of the glory of God.   ROMANS 5:1–2

Who shall separate us from the love of Christ? Shall tribulation, or distress, or persecution, or famine, or nakedness, or peril, or sword? As it is written: "For Your sake we are killed all day long; we are accounted as sheep for the slaughter." Yet in all these things we are more than conquerors through Him who loved us. For I am persuaded that neither death nor life, nor angels nor principalities nor powers, nor things present nor things to come, nor height nor depth, nor any other created thing, shall be able to separate us from the love of God which is in Christ Jesus our Lord.
                              ROMANS 8:35–39

Do you not know that you are the temple of God and that the Spirit of God dwells in you? If anyone defiles the temple of God, God will destroy him. For the temple of God is holy, which temple you are.   1 CORINTHIANS 3:16–17

Or do you not know that your body is the temple of the Holy Spirit who is in you, whom you have from God, and you are not your own? For you were bought at a price; therefore glorify God in your body and in your spirit, which are God's.

1 CORINTHIANS 6:19–20

For you are all sons of God through faith in Christ Jesus. For as many of you as were baptized into Christ have put on Christ.   GALATIANS 3:26–27

Blessed be the God and Father of our Lord Jesus Christ, who has blessed us with every spiritual blessing in the heavenly places in Christ, just as He chose us in Him before the foundation of the world, that we should be holy and without blame before Him in love, having predestined us to adoption as sons by Jesus Christ to Himself, according to the good pleasure of His will, to the praise of the glory of His grace, by which He has made us accepted in the Beloved. In Him we have redemption through His blood, the forgiveness of sins, according to the riches of His grace which He made to abound toward us in all wisdom and prudence.

EPHESIANS 1:3–8

Giving thanks to the Father who has qualified us to be partakers of the inheritance of the saints in the light. He has delivered us from the power of darkness and conveyed us into the kingdom of the Son of His love, in whom we have redemption through His blood, the forgiveness of sins.

COLOSSIANS 1:12–14

But now in Christ Jesus you who once were far off have been brought near by the blood of Christ.

EPHESIANS 2:13

And you, being dead in your trespasses and the uncircumcision of your flesh, He has made alive together with Him, having forgiven you all trespasses, having wiped out the handwriting of requirements that was against us, which was contrary to us. And He has taken it out of the way, having nailed it to the cross.   COLOSSIANS 2:13–14

I write to you, little children, because your sins are forgiven you for His name's sake. I write to you, fathers, because you have known Him who is from the beginning. I write to you, young men, because you have overcome the wicked one. I write to you, little children, because you have known the Father. I have written to you, fathers, because you have known Him who is from the beginning. I have written to you, young men, because you are strong, and the word of God abides in you, and you have overcome the wicked one.   1 JOHN 2:12–14

But you are a chosen generation, a royal priesthood, a holy nation, His own special people, that you may proclaim the praises of Him who called you out of darkness into His marvelous light.

1 PETER 2:9

Blessed be the God and Father of our Lord Jesus Christ, who according to His abundant mercy has begotten us again to a living hope through the resurrection of Jesus Christ from the dead, to an inheritance incorruptible and undefiled and that does not fade away, reserved in heaven for you, who are kept by the power of God through faith for salvation ready to be revealed in the last time.

1 PETER 1:3–5

These are only a few samples of the tone of every epistle. Notice the assured expressions "has blessed," "have redemption," "has made us accepted." Notice, also, the present tense of possession continually used: "are," "have," "has," "is." Never once is there a "hope so" or "perhaps so" or "I wish it might be so." Unquestioning, rejoicing assurance breathes from every word.

THE WONDERFUL RESULTS OF ASSURANCE

All exhortations to be holy, as well as all exhortations to serve, are based on this assured knowledge of our reconciliation with God.

Therefore, having these promises, beloved, let us cleanse ourselves from all filthiness of the flesh and spirit, perfecting holiness in the fear of God.
2 CORINTHIANS 7:1

I beseech you therefore, brethren, by the mercies of God, that you present your bodies a living sacrifice, holy, acceptable to God, which is your reasonable service. ROMANS 12:1

We are not to be holy in order to gain the promises, but because we *have* the promises.

Set your mind on things above, not on things on the earth. For you died, and your life is hidden with Christ in God. When Christ who is our life appears, then you also will appear with Him in glory. Therefore put to death your members which

are on the earth: fornication, uncleanness, passion,
evil desire, and covetousness, which is idolatry.

COLOSSIANS 3:2–5

And do not grieve the Holy Spirit of God, by whom
you were sealed for the day of redemption. Let all
bitterness, wrath, anger, clamor, and evil speaking
be put away from you, with all malice. And be kind
to one another, tenderhearted, forgiving one another, just as God in Christ forgave you.

EPHESIANS 4:30–32

Behold what manner of love the Father has bestowed on us, that we should be called children of
God! Therefore the world does not know us, because it did not know Him. Beloved, now we are
children of God; and it has not yet been revealed
what we shall be, but we know that when He is revealed, we shall be like Him, for we shall see Him
as He is. And everyone who has this hope in Him
purifies himself, just as He is pure.   1 JOHN 3:1–3

God wants from us the service of a son, not of a
servant only. A servant works for wages; a son works
out of love. A servant labors to gain something; a son
labors because all has been given to him. But how
can we render a son's service unless we know that
we *are* sons?

Therefore be imitators of God as dear children.
And walk in love, as Christ also has loved us and
given Himself for us, an offering and a sacrifice
to God for a sweet-smelling aroma.

EPHESIANS 5:1–2

Therefore you are no longer a slave but a son, and if a son, then an heir of God through Christ.

GALATIANS 4:7

JUST FAITH IN THE FACTS

Therefore, since we have indisputably proved that assurance of salvation is the only normal condition of a child of God, our next point must be to show how this assurance is to be arrived at.

It comes simply by believing God. He says certain things about Himself and about us. Faith believes these things, and assurance follows. Notice that, in the Scriptures, believing and having are always joined together. "He who believes has" is the continual declaration!

[Jesus said,] "Most assuredly, I say to you, he who believes in Me has everlasting life." JOHN 6:47

[Jesus said,] "And as Moses lifted up the serpent in the wilderness, even so must the Son of Man be lifted up, that whoever believes in Him should not perish but have eternal life. For God so loved the world that He gave His only begotten Son, that whoever believes in Him should not perish but have everlasting life. For God did not send His Son into the world to condemn the world, but that the world through Him might be saved. He who believes in Him is not condemned; but he who does not believe is condemned already, because he has not believed in the name of the only begotten Son of God." JOHN 3:14–18

He who believes in the Son has everlasting life; and he who does not believe the Son shall not see life, but the wrath of God abides on him.   JOHN 3:36

[Jesus said,] "Most assuredly, I say to you, he who hears My word and believes in Him who sent Me has everlasting life, and shall not come into judgment, but has passed from death into life."
                                                                JOHN 5:24

But as many as received Him, to them He gave the right to become children of God, to those who believe in His name.   JOHN 1:12

And Jesus said to them, "I am the bread of life. He who comes to Me shall never hunger, and he who believes in Me shall never thirst."   JOHN 6:35

[Jesus said,] "And this is the will of Him who sent Me, that everyone who sees the Son and believes in Him may have everlasting life; and I will raise him up at the last day."   JOHN 6:40

Jesus said to her, "I am the resurrection and the life. He who believes in Me, though he may die, he shall live. And whoever lives and believes in Me shall never die. Do you believe this?"
                                                                JOHN 11:25–26

And truly Jesus did many other signs in the presence of His disciples, which are not written in this book; but these are written that you may believe that Jesus is the Christ, the Son of God, and that believing you may have life in His name.
                                                                JOHN 20:30–31

Notice that the Bible never says, "He who feels has," but always, "He who believes has." Our feelings are no guide here whatsoever. In all matters of fact, it is foolish to depend on feelings. We certainly never rely on them in our earthly affairs. We never say over a piece of good news or bad news, "Do I feel that it is true?" but we limit ourselves simply to the question, "Is it true?"

Who would be so silly as to enter a railroad station, take the first train available, and then sit down and try to "feel" whether it was the right train or not? We all know that the state of our feelings could not alter the facts, and our sole aim in such cases is always to find out the facts.

To obtain assurance of salvation, then, we must not depend on our feelings, but must simply find out the facts.

God's order, and the order of good common sense, is always, (1) Fact, (2) Faith, (3) Feeling. But in matters of religion, man reverses this order and says, (1) Feeling, (2) Faith, (3) Fact.

In the case of the train, we would find peace and assurance by asking someone who knew and by believing his word. Likewise, in the case of our relationship with the Lord, we must hear and believe what God says about it, without regard to how we feel.

If we receive the witness of men, the witness of God is greater; for this is the witness of God which He has testified of His Son. He who believes in the Son of God has the witness in himself; he who does not believe God has made Him a liar, because he has not believed the testimony that God has given

of His Son. And this is the testimony: that God has given us eternal life, and this life is in His Son.
1 JOHN 5:9–11

We receive "the witness of men" continually without a question or a doubt. Should we be less ready to receive "the witness of God"? In verse 10, notice that it is not "He who has the witness in himself will believe," but "He who believes…has the witness in himself." Here we have: first, the fact; second, the faith; third, the feeling.

What are we to do, then, in order to get assurance of salvation?

Then they said to Him, "What shall we do, that we may work the works of God?" Jesus answered and said to them, "This is the work of God, that you believe in Him whom He sent."   JOHN 6:28–29

We must believe two things: first, what God says concerning Christ; second, what God says concerning us.

It is not really believing a person if we believe only half of what he says. Yet many who would consider it the worst of sins to doubt God's testimony concerning Christ, consider it no sin at all, but in fact rather virtuous humility, to doubt His testimony concerning themselves. They dare not question that Jesus is the Christ but find no difficulty in doubting whether they themselves are born of God. Yet God joins the two inseparably together.

Whoever believes that Jesus is the Christ is born of God.   1 JOHN 5:1

Here is a plain and simple statement. "Whoever believes...is born"—not "will be," but "is," this very moment. No one can believe who is not born of God.

But you may say, How can I know that I believe? Could you write on a piece of paper "I do not believe that Jesus is the Christ" and sign your name? Would it not be a lie if you were to do so? If the alternatives were presented to you of denying Christ or going to prison, would you not choose prison?

You do believe, therefore, that Jesus is the Christ, and God says that whoever believes *is* born of Him. Does this fact not settle the question?

Whoever confesses that Jesus is the Son of God, God abides in him, and he in God.   1 JOHN 4:15

Could language be plainer than this? If you confess that Jesus is the Son of God, God dwells in you right now.

But what does it say? "The word is near you, in your mouth and in your heart" (that is, the word of faith which we preach): that if you confess with your mouth the Lord Jesus and believe in your heart that God has raised Him from the dead, you will be saved.   ROMANS 10:8–9

What would we think of a child who would doubt whether he was really his mother's own child, who would say, "Well, I have a trembling hope that I am, but that is all"? Would not such statements be equivalent to casting a doubt on the mother's word? And do not our doubts as to whether we are really God's children make Him out to be a liar?

He who does not believe God has made Him a liar, because he has not believed the testimony that God has given of His Son. And this is the testimony: that God has given us eternal life, and this life is in His Son.   1 JOHN 5:10–11

The record we are to believe is that "God has given us eternal life." If He has given it, we must have it, and there is nothing more to be said about it.

These things I have written to you who believe in the name of the Son of God, that you may know that you have eternal life, and that you may continue to believe in the name of the Son of God.
                                1 JOHN 5:13

We *have* eternal life if we believe, but we may not *know* that we have it, and our peace depends on our knowing it. A man may have a fortune left to him by a friend, but until he knows the fact, he cannot enjoy the fortune.

Assurance of salvation, therefore, is simply the "knowing" of which John speaks. This assurance arises from our belief in the trustworthy testimony, not of our feelings, but of God's Word.

And truly Jesus did many other signs in the presence of His disciples, which are not written in this book; but these are written that you may believe that Jesus is the Christ, the Son of God, and that believing you may have life in His name.
                                JOHN 20:30–31

Not what we feel, but what the record is; not what our experiences are, but what has been "written"—this is the foundation for assurance of salvation.

All of us know the strange experience of being "turned around" when walking on the streets of a city or traveling on a train—when we feel as if we were going in one direction, although in fact we are going in exactly the opposite direction. Our feelings in this case contradict the facts, and even though we may even know this, it is almost impossible not to yield to these feelings and take the wrong direction. When I *feel* that I am going north, for example, yet know as a *fact* that I am going south, I have discovered that I can conquer these feelings and turn myself around right by just repeating to myself in a very emphatic way, "I am, I *am*, I AM going south." In a minute or two, my feelings always come under the control of the fact, and I begin to feel, as well as to know, that I really am going south.

In the same way, when we have convinced ourselves from God's "testimony" (1 John 5:10) that our sins are forgiven and that our peace is made with God, we can control our feeling that it is not so by a similar process. We can assert on the authority of God's Word, "My sins *are* forgiven; I *am* God's child; God *is* reconciled to me; I *am* a Christian."

Persevering in such a course, regardless of feelings, will always bring peace and deliverance to every soul that is willing to take God at His Word and to risk all on His trustworthiness.

Chapter 5

The Keeping Power of God

Behold, I am with you and will keep you wherever you go, and will bring you back to this land; for I will not leave you until I have done what I have spoken to you.
—Genesis 28:15

All of us feel the need of being kept by a power outside ourselves. Life is full of dangers to both soul and body, and most of the time we are too blind to see them. We are like little, helpless, ignorant children, walking in strange pathways and knowing nothing of the traps and pitfalls that await our unwary steps.

We need to cry out continually with the psalmist,

But my eyes are upon You, O GOD the Lord; in You I take refuge; do not leave my soul destitute. Keep me from the snares they have laid for me, and from the traps of the workers of iniquity.
PSALM 141:8–9

And continually we have the Lord's answer:

> For He shall give His angels charge over you, to keep you in all your ways. In their hands they shall bear you up, lest you dash your foot against a stone. You shall tread upon the lion and the cobra, the young lion and the serpent you shall trample underfoot.   PSALM 91:11–13

> Then you will walk safely in your way, and your foot will not stumble. When you lie down, you will not be afraid; yes, you will lie down and your sleep will be sweet. Do not be afraid of sudden terror, nor of trouble from the wicked when it comes; for the LORD will be your confidence, and will keep your foot from being caught.   PROVERBS 3:23–26

THE LORD HOLDS US AND KEEPS US

The Lord is like a mother who holds the hand of her little child as they walk together to keep him from stumbling over the obstacles that lie in his way. It is the mother's holding the child that makes him safe, not the child's holding the mother.

Notice the words "bear you up" in the passage above. They can be illustrated by the infant in the mother's arms, safe because of her upholding. His little frightened grasps when danger is near do not make him any safer, for his safety rests in the fact that his mother holds him. Everything depends on whether *she* is able to keep him safe.

> Now to Him who is able to keep you from stumbling, and to present you faultless before the presence of His glory with exceeding joy.   JUDE 24

Mothers are not always able to keep their children from falling, but God is. Perhaps you say, as others have said in their ignorance, "If I were to get religion, I'm afraid I couldn't keep it." This is true, you could not. But if you let God get you, He will keep you.

I, the LORD, keep it, I water it every moment; lest any hurt it, I keep it night and day.   ISAIAH 27:3

Our hearts are like a garden that is open on every side to enemies, who are pressing in to ravage and destroy. There is no safety for us except in the keeping power of the divine Gardener, who neither slumbers nor sleeps (Psalm 121:4), whom no enemy can either elude or conquer.

Hear the word of the LORD, O nations, and declare it in the isles afar off, and say, "He who scattered Israel will gather him, and keep him as a shepherd does his flock."   JEREMIAH 31:10

We are like poor helpless sheep who have no armor against their enemies, and no wisdom to save them from danger. But we have a divine Shepherd to care for us; therefore, we need not fear.

For the Lord's portion is His people; Jacob is the place of His inheritance. He found him in a desert land and in the wasteland, a howling wilderness; He encircled him, He instructed him, He kept him as the apple of His eye.   DEUTERONOMY 32:9–10

Nothing is dearer to a man, or more tenderly cared for, than the apple (the pupil) of his eye. Since we are to the Lord like "the apple of His eye," we can be sure of the tenderest divine keeping.

Show Your marvelous lovingkindness by Your right hand, O You who save those who trust in You from those who rise up against them. Keep me as the apple of Your eye.   PSALM 17:7–8

THE BIG "IF"

Hide me under the shadow of Your wings, from the wicked who oppress me, from my deadly enemies who surround me.   PSALM 17:8–9

As the mother hen keeps her little chicks under the shadow of her wings, so the Lord will keep us, *if* we will let Him. But this is a very big *if*. What would we think of a little chick that stood off by itself, trembling with fright when danger was near, saying, "I am not worthy to go under my mother's wing. I am too little, too weak, and too insignificant. I must wait until I am stronger and more worthy of her love"? Would the mother hen not answer such a foolish little chick by saying, "It is just because you are little and weak that I am spreading out my wings to cover you and am clucking for you to come. If you were big and strong I would not invite you. Your littleness and your weakness are your claim to my care."
Is there nothing in this parable to teach us a lesson?

He who dwells in the secret place of the Most High shall abide under the shadow of the Almighty. I will say of the LORD, "He is my refuge and my fortress; my God, in Him I will trust." Surely He shall deliver you from the snare of the fowler and from the perilous pestilence. He shall cover you with His feathers, and under His wings you shall take refuge; His truth shall be your shield and buckler. You shall not be afraid of the terror by night, nor of the arrow that flies by day, nor of the pestilence that walks in darkness, nor of the destruction that lays waste at noonday. A thousand may fall at your side, and ten thousand at your right hand; but it shall not come near you. Only with your eyes shall you look, and see the reward of the wicked. Because you have made the LORD, who is my refuge, even the Most High, your dwelling place, no evil shall befall you, nor shall any plague come near your dwelling.

PSALM 91:1–10

Have we ever said, or at least thought, that we were too weak and unworthy to make the Lord our refuge? Have we not sometimes in our hearts planned to seek this refuge when we felt more worthy of entering it?

My help comes from the LORD, who made heaven and earth. He will not allow your foot to be moved; He who keeps you will not slumber. Behold, He who keeps Israel shall neither slumber nor sleep. The LORD is your keeper; the LORD is your shade at your right hand. The sun shall not strike you by day, nor the moon by night. The LORD shall preserve you from all evil; He shall preserve your soul. The LORD shall preserve your going out and your coming in from this time forth, and even forevermore.

PSALM 121:2–8

This psalm could be called "The Bible Keep."
The keep was the strongest and best protected room
in an ancient castle, the one that would be the last to
be reached by any enemy. In this keep, all the sick
and weak and helpless residents of the castle were
hidden in every time of danger. The qualification for
entrance was, simply and only, need and weakness.
How foolish, then, it would have been for any to
have made their weakness the reason for remaining
outside! Yet how continually this is done regarding
the Lord's keep.

The LORD preserves the simple; I was brought low,
and He saved me. Return to your rest, O my soul,
for the LORD has dealt bountifully with you. For
You have delivered my soul from death, my eyes
from tears, and my feet from falling.

PSALM 116:6–8

It is the weak, "the simple," those who are
"brought low" whom the Lord preserves.

BETTER THAN A HUMAN KEEPER

Notice the fact that this divine Keeper never
slumbers or sleeps (Psalm 121:4), and therefore
never neglects those for whom He cares. Think of
the fatal consequences of neglect on the part of the
keepers of a prison, the keepers of a flock of sheep,
or the keepers of a dangerous military outpost. Observe, by contrast, what sort of a keeper our Lord is.

We all realize the responsibilities of a human
keeper when anything has been committed to his
care. When we are given anything to keep, we feel

that we must care for that thing more than we care for our own possessions. If we have these high ideals of responsibility in our own case, how much more must the divine Keeper have them!

[Jesus said,] "Now I am no longer in the world, but these are in the world, and I come to You. Holy Father, keep through Your name those whom You have given Me, that they may be one as We are. While I was with them in the world, I kept them in Your name. Those whom You gave Me I have kept; and none of them is lost except the son of perdition, that the Scripture might be fulfilled."

JOHN 17:11–12

[Jesus said,] "For I have come down from heaven, not to do My own will, but the will of Him who sent Me. This is the will of the Father who sent Me, that of all He has given Me I should lose nothing, but should raise it up at the last day."

JOHN 6:38–39

We may, therefore, commit ourselves with the utmost confidence to the keeping of the Lord.

Therefore let those who suffer according to the will of God commit their souls to Him in doing good, as to a faithful Creator. 1 PETER 4:19

Our Creator is our Keeper, and He is "a faithful Creator." People whom we trust often prove unfaithful, but He never will! If we are grieved when people doubt our faithfulness in any matter committed to us, how much more must He be grieved!

But the Lord is faithful, who will establish you and guard you from the evil one. 2 THESSALONIANS 3:3

Thus says God the LORD, who created the heavens and stretched them out, who spread forth the earth and that which comes from it, who gives breath to the people on it, and spirit to those who walk on it: "I, the LORD, have called You in righteousness, and will hold Your hand; I will keep You and give You as a covenant to the people, as a light to the Gentiles." ISAIAH 42:5–6

Therefore, Paul could say,

For this reason I also suffer these things; nevertheless I am not ashamed, for I know whom I have believed and am persuaded that He is able to keep what I have committed to Him until that Day.
2 TIMOTHY 1:12

THE SECRET OF CONFIDENCE

If we know Him, we cannot fail to trust Him. No one who knows Him ever did yet. And this, after all, is the true secret of confidence—knowledge of the trustworthiness of the one to be trusted. We act on this knowledge in our earthly affairs, for we are never so silly as to look inside ourselves to see whether we can or ought to trust someone else. We look at the other person instead and try to find out his character and his ways.

But in their interaction with the Lord, many people act on an entirely different principle. They look at themselves for a basis of trust instead of at

Him. They behold self and its untrustworthiness and are filled with doubts and despair, whereas a single look at Him would fill them with perfect peace, because of His utter trustworthiness.

> You will keep him in perfect peace, whose mind is stayed on You, because he trusts in You.
>
> ISAIAH 26:3

Consider the words "perfect peace." They are illustrated by the peace that comes when we have entrusted any precious thing to someone for safekeeping. Take a bank, for instance. Think of how we are continually trusting banks, and how comfortable we feel when we have transferred our money from our own keeping to that of some safe bank. How foolish it would be to run back to the bank every hour to see if our money is safe! In the same way, how foolish it is to doubt God! When we imagine how indignant the bank officers would be at such behavior, we see how our doubts and fears must grieve our God.

THREE ESSENTIAL INGREDIENTS

In every stage of the spiritual life, our part in this divine keeping is threefold. We must yield, trust, and obey.

> Therefore submit to God. Resist the devil and he will flee from you.   JAMES 4:7

> Oh, how great is Your goodness, which You have laid up for those who fear You, which You have

prepared for those who trust in You in the presence of the sons of men! You shall hide them in the secret place of Your presence from the plots of man; You shall keep them secretly in a pavilion from the strife of tongues. PSALM 31:19–20

Keep my soul, and deliver me; let me not be ashamed, for I put my trust in You. PSALM 25:20

There can be no keeping without yielding and trusting. In the nature of things, a keeper must have that which he is to keep. It must be entrusted entirely to his care.

Nor can there be any keeping without obedience.

My son, keep your father's command, and do not forsake the law of your mother. Bind them continually upon your heart; tie them around your neck. When you roam, they will lead you; when you sleep, they will keep you; and when you awake, they will speak with you. For the commandment is a lamp, and the law a light; reproofs of instruction are the way of life, to keep you from the evil woman, from the flattering tongue of a seductress. PROVERBS 6:20–24

He also taught me, and said to me: "Let your heart retain my words; keep my commands, and live. Get wisdom! Get understanding! Do not forget, nor turn away from the words of my mouth. Do not forsake her, and she will preserve you; love her, and she will keep you." PROVERBS 4:4–6

Therefore you shall keep the commandment, the statutes, and the judgments which I command you today, to observe them. Then it shall come to pass, because you listen to these judgments, and keep and do them, that the LORD your God will keep with you the covenant and the mercy which He swore to your fathers.   DEUTERONOMY 7:11–12

FOLLOWING THE LEADER

If we want to be kept, we must be guided, and we must follow that guidance.

Behold, I send an Angel before you to keep you in the way and to bring you into the place which I have prepared.   EXODUS 23:20

And you shall remember that the LORD your God led you all the way these forty years in the wilderness, to humble you and test you, to know what was in your heart, whether you would keep His commandments or not. So He humbled you, allowed you to hunger, and fed you with manna which you did not know nor did your fathers know, that He might make you know that man shall not live by bread alone; but man lives by every word that proceeds from the mouth of the LORD. Your garments did not wear out on you, nor did your foot swell these forty years. You should know in your heart that as a man chastens his son, so the LORD your God chastens you. Therefore you shall keep the commandments of the LORD your God, to walk in His ways and to fear Him.
                              DEUTERONOMY 8:2–6

For the LORD our God is He who brought us and our fathers up out of the land of Egypt, from the

house of bondage, who did those great signs in our
sight, and preserved us in all the way that we went
and among all the people through whom we passed.

JOSHUA 24:17

HAVE IT GOD'S WAY

We are tempted to think that it is not true
keeping unless the keeping is done in our own way
and according to our own ideas. But our Lord Himself has taught us that our keeping must be done in
God's way and not our own, or it would not be true
keeping at all.

Then he [Satan] brought Him to Jerusalem, set
Him on the pinnacle of the temple, and said to
Him, "If You are the Son of God, throw Yourself
down from here. For it is written: 'He shall give
His angels charge over you, to keep you,' and, 'In
their hands they shall bear you up, lest you dash
your foot against a stone.'" And Jesus answered
and said to him, "It has been said, 'You shall not
tempt the LORD your God.'"   LUKE 4:9–12

Only God, who knows the end of things from the
beginning, can keep us. If it seems that He has left
us to the will of our enemies for a time, it is only so
that He may bring us to a grander victory in the end.
We are not to be taken out of the world and its trials,
but we are to be kept in the midst of these trials and
be preserved from the evil that is in them.

[Jesus said,] "I do not pray that You should take
them out of the world, but that You should keep
them from the evil one."   JOHN 17:15

[You] are kept by the power of God through faith for salvation ready to be revealed in the last time. In this you greatly rejoice, though now for a little while, if need be, you have been grieved by various trials, that the genuineness of your faith, being much more precious than gold that perishes, though it is tested by fire, may be found to praise, honor, and glory at the revelation of Jesus Christ.

1 PETER 1:5-7

Because you have kept My command to persevere, I also will keep you from the hour of trial which shall come upon the whole world, to test those who dwell on the earth.   REVELATION 3:10

GOD'S PATH TO PEACE

The divine pathway by which we may enter this heavenly keep, even while we are here on earth, is plainly set before us.

Be anxious for nothing, but in everything by prayer and supplication, with thanksgiving, let your requests be made known to God; and the peace of God, which surpasses all understanding, will guard [the Greek word for guard means "will guard as with a garrison"] your hearts and minds through Christ Jesus.   PHILIPPIANS 4:6-7

We must give up all our concerns by a complete surrender of ourselves and all we have to the divine Keeper, and by an implicit trust in Him. Then we must simply let Him know our wants and our needs from day to day. If we honestly follow this course and persist in it steadfastly, the result will unfailingly be that the peace of God will keep, as with a garrison, our hearts and minds.

I remember once hearing of a man who thought he could not live unless he kept himself alive. He was afraid his breath would stop if he did not keep it going by his own efforts. He tried so hard to keep breathing that he nearly strangled himself in the struggle. In great alarm, his family called in a physician, who, seeing the difficulty, ordered him to stop trying to breathe. "I will die if I do," gasped out the poor man. "Die, then," exclaimed the doctor, "but STOP!" The man, conquered by the voice of authority, obeyed. The moment he stopped trying to breathe, his breath came easily and without effort.

It is the same way with some Christians. They are trying to keep themselves alive, and their life is nearly strangled in the effort. If they would just give up trying to live and would let Christ keep them alive, they would find themselves living easily and without effort.

Chapter 6

Rest for the Soul

Come to Me, all you who labor and are heavy laden,
and I will give you rest.
—Matthew 11:28

There is in every human heart a cry for rest. In
our earthly stage of existence, life at its best is
full of weariness. Both soul and body "labor and are
heavy laden" with their struggles, and humanity
makes one long moan for rest.

> My heart is severely pained within me, and the
> terrors of death have fallen upon me. Fearfulness
> and trembling have come upon me, and horror has
> overwhelmed me. So I said, "Oh, that I had wings
> like a dove! I would fly away and be at rest. In-
> deed, I would wander far off, and remain in the
> wilderness....I would hasten my escape from the
> windy storm and tempest."   PSALM 55:4–8

We would gladly "fly away" if we could, but we
cannot. Therefore, the rest our Lord proposes is not
a rest from the trial and struggle, but a rest in it.

Rest in the LORD, and wait patiently for Him; do
not fret because of him who prospers in his way,
because of the man who brings wicked schemes to
pass.   PSALM 37:7

We are to "rest in the LORD," not in circumstances or things or people. This rest takes the
"fret" out of life. This resting in God is to the soul
what resting in a bed is to the body. We all know the
delightful relaxing of every strain that comes to us
in bed—the delicious letting go of the whole body in
a perfect abandonment to ease and comfort. Such is
the ease of soul that comes from resting "in the
LORD."

But this rest implies perfect confidence in Him.
If a person were to lie down on a bed that was in any
way insecure and was therefore liable to fall, it
would be impossible for him to let himself go in an
abandonment to rest. He would be compelled to hold
on to something in order to keep himself safe in such
a bed as that.

It must be because Christians do not really believe the Lord alone to be a perfectly secure resting
place that they seek so eagerly for something else to
hold on to—some good feelings, some good works,
some church ordinances, or some remarkable experiences.

What would we think of a man who was afraid
his bed could not support him and therefore tried to
hold himself up by ropes attached to the ceiling? We
would think him foolish indeed. Yet this would be
nothing compared with the foolishness of those
Christians who say they are resting in Christ but, at
the same time, are holding on to other supports.

REST IS AVAILABLE FOR YOU

The work of righteousness will be peace, and the effect of righteousness, quietness and assurance forever. My people will dwell in a peaceful habitation, in secure dwellings, and in quiet resting places.   ISAIAH 32:17–18

Christ is a resting place that cannot fail. To those who have come to Him, there ought to be no fear of falling, and no strain to keep oneself safe.

My people have been lost sheep. Their shepherds have led them astray; they have turned them away on the mountains. They have gone from mountain to hill; they have forgotten their resting place.
                    JEREMIAH 50:6

Truly, God's people have "forgotten their resting place"! The almost universal restlessness of those who claim to be believers testifies to this fact. The result is as grievous to us now as it was to Israel of old.

For thus says the Lord GOD, the Holy One of Israel: "In returning and rest you shall be saved; in quietness and confidence shall be your strength." But you would not, and you said, "No, for we will flee on horses"; therefore you shall flee! And, "We will ride on swift horses"; therefore those who pursue you shall be swift!   ISAIAH 30:15–16

To [His people] He said, "This is the rest with which you may cause the weary to rest," and, "This is the refreshing"; yet they would not hear.
                    ISAIAH 28:12

This blessed rest, however, always awaits God's people, whoever and wherever they may be, and no past unrest can serve to hinder us from now entering in.

There remains therefore a rest for the people of God.   HEBREWS 4:9

"Therefore do not fear, O My servant Jacob," says the LORD, "nor be dismayed, O Israel; for behold, I will save you from afar, and your seed from the land of their captivity. Jacob shall return, have rest and be quiet, and no one shall make him afraid."   JEREMIAH 30:10

TRUSTING, NOT TRYING

This rest can be entered into only by faith. In the nature of things, unbelief completely shuts us out.

And to whom did He swear that they would not enter His rest, but to those who did not obey? So we see that they could not enter in because of unbelief. Therefore, since a promise remains of entering His rest, let us fear lest any of you seem to have come short of it. For indeed the gospel was preached to us as well as to them; but the word which they heard did not profit them, not being mixed with faith in those who heard it.
                                    HEBREWS 3:18–4:2

Notice the expressions "entering" and "enter in." We can neither work for this rest nor purchase it; we simply "enter" the rest provided for us by One who offers Himself to us as our resting place. Just as we rest in a strong and loving earthly friend who undertakes our case and promises to carry it through, so, only infinitely more, must we rest in the Lord. Faith is required on our part in both cases alike. If we doubt our friend, we cannot rest, no matter how much we may try; and if we doubt our Lord, we cannot rest either, no matter how much we may try. Rest always comes by trusting, not by trying.

For we who have believed do enter that rest, as He has said: "So I swore in My wrath, 'They shall not enter My rest,'" although the works were finished from the foundation of the world. For He has spoken in a certain place of the seventh day in this way: "And God rested on the seventh day from all His works"; and again in this place: "They shall not enter My rest." Since therefore it remains that some must enter it, and those to whom it was first preached did not enter because of disobedience, again He designates a certain day, saying in David, "Today," after such a long time, as it has been said: "Today, if you will hear His voice, do not harden your hearts." For if Joshua had given them rest, then He would not afterward have spoken of another day. There remains therefore a rest for the people of God. For he who has entered His rest has himself also ceased from his works as God did from His. Let us therefore be diligent ["labour" KJV] to enter that rest, lest anyone fall according to the same example of disobedience.

HEBREWS 4:3–11

The "labour" to enter into rest is not the labor to work, but the labor to cease from our own working.

The natural thought of the human heart is that salvation is to be gained by our own self-efforts, and it is indeed often a "labour" to get rid of this thinking.

THE SABBATH AS A TYPE

Soul Rest

Let us look again at Hebrews 4:9:

There remains therefore a rest for the people of God.

Next to this verse, in the marginal notes of my Bible, "rest" is rendered "keeping of a Sabbath." This note teaches what true soul rest is by using a type. A type is a person or thing in the Old Testament that foreshadows another person or thing in the New Testament.

Thus the heavens and the earth, and all the host of them, were finished. And on the seventh day God ended His work which He had done, and He rested on the seventh day from all His work which He had done. Then God blessed the seventh day and sanctified it, because in it He rested from all His work which God had created and made.
GENESIS 2:1–3

And the LORD spoke to Moses, saying, "Speak also to the children of Israel, saying: 'Surely My Sabbaths you shall keep, for it is a sign between Me and you throughout your generations, that you may know that I am the LORD who sanctifies you.

You shall keep the Sabbath, therefore, for it is holy to you. Everyone who profanes it shall surely be put to death; for whoever does any work on it, that person shall be cut off from among his people. Work shall be done for six days, but the seventh is the Sabbath of rest, holy to the LORD. Whoever does any work on the Sabbath day, he shall surely be put to death. Therefore the children of Israel shall keep the Sabbath, to observe the Sabbath throughout their generations as a perpetual covenant. It is a sign between Me and the children of Israel forever; for in six days the LORD made the heavens and the earth, and on the seventh day He rested and was refreshed.'"   EXODUS 31:12–17

What this outward Sabbath was to the children of Israel, the inward keeping of a Sabbath is to be to us now. We are to cease from our own works inwardly, as they were to cease from their own works outwardly.

Now it happened that some of the people went out on the seventh day to gather, but they found none. And the LORD said to Moses, "How long do you refuse to keep My commandments and My laws? See! For the LORD has given you the Sabbath; therefore He gives you on the sixth day bread for two days. Let every man remain in his place; let no man go out of his place on the seventh day." So the people rested on the seventh day.   EXODUS 16:27–30

The Sabbath was a *gift*, not a *demand*. The Lord had provided the supply for that day; therefore, they did not need to seek for any more but were commanded to rest instead.

Now while the children of Israel were in the wilderness, they found a man gathering sticks on the Sabbath day. And those who found him gathering sticks brought him to Moses and Aaron, and to all the congregation. They put him under guard, because it had not been explained what should be done to him. Then the LORD said to Moses, "The man must surely be put to death; all the congregation shall stone him with stones outside the camp." So, as the LORD commanded Moses, all the congregation brought him outside the camp and stoned him with stones, and he died.

NUMBERS 15:32–36

This is a type of the spiritual death that comes upon the soul that breaks God's inward Sabbath of rest, that legally depends on self-efforts for salvation.

Someone Who Works for Us and Carries Our Burdens

For he who has entered His rest has himself also ceased from his works as God did from His.

HEBREWS 4:10

God rested because He had finished His work. We are to rest because the Lord works for us. Everything is provided for us in Christ, and we are to enter into the results of His labor and be at rest.

Thus says the LORD: "Take heed to yourselves, and bear no burden on the Sabbath day, nor bring it in by the gates of Jerusalem; nor carry a burden out of your houses on the Sabbath day, nor do any work, but hallow the Sabbath day, as I commanded your fathers." JEREMIAH 17:21–22

In this inward "keeping of a Sabbath," we are not to bear burdens, because the Lord bears them for us.

Cast your burden on the LORD, and He shall sustain you; He shall never permit the righteous to be moved. PSALM 55:22

But if you will not heed Me to hallow the Sabbath day, such as not carrying a burden when entering the gates of Jerusalem on the Sabbath day, then I will kindle a fire in its gates, and it shall devour the palaces of Jerusalem, and it shall not be quenched. JEREMIAH 17:27

Some people may experience the natural fear that nothing will be accomplished for the soul that thus keeps a continual inward Sabbath and bears no burdens. But the answer to this anxiety is full and glorious:

"And it shall be, if you heed Me carefully," says the LORD, "to bring no burden through the gates of this city on the Sabbath day, but hallow the Sabbath day, to do no work in it, then shall enter the gates of this city kings and princes sitting on the throne of David, riding in chariots and on horses, they and their princes, accompanied by the men of Judah and the inhabitants of Jerusalem; and this city shall remain forever. And they shall come from the cities of Judah and from the places around Jerusalem, from the land of Benjamin and from the lowland, from the mountains and from the South, bringing burnt offerings and sacrifices, grain offerings and incense, bringing sacrifices of praise to the house of the LORD."

JEREMIAH 17:24–26

If you turn away your foot from the Sabbath, from doing your pleasure on My holy day, and call the Sabbath a delight, the holy day of the LORD honorable, and shall honor Him, not doing your own ways, nor finding your own pleasure, nor speaking your own words, then you shall delight yourself in the LORD; and I will cause you to ride on the high hills of the earth, and feed you with the heritage of Jacob your father. The mouth of the LORD has spoken.

ISAIAH 58:13–14

Plentiful blessings, full of richness, come to the soul that thus ceases from its own works and lets God work for it. When we bear our own burdens and do our own work, deadness and loss are the result. When we rest in the Lord, riches and victory follow.

This truth is further illustrated by the Sabbath of the seventh year, which the Israelites were commanded to keep, and the Sabbath of the Year of Jubilee, which they were to observe every fiftieth year.

And the LORD spoke to Moses on Mount Sinai, saying, "Speak to the children of Israel, and say to them: 'When you come into the land which I give you, then the land shall keep a sabbath to the LORD. Six years you shall sow your field, and six years you shall prune your vineyard, and gather its fruit; but in the seventh year there shall be a sabbath of solemn rest for the land, a sabbath to the LORD. You shall neither sow your field nor prune your vineyard. What grows of its own accord of your harvest you shall not reap, nor gather the grapes of your untended vine, for it is a year of rest for the land.'"   LEVITICUS 25:1–5

And the LORD spoke to Moses on Mount Sinai, saying, "...And you shall count seven sabbaths of years for yourself, seven times seven years; and the time of the seven sabbaths of years shall be to you forty-nine years. Then you shall cause the trumpet of the Jubilee to sound on the tenth day of the seventh month; on the Day of Atonement you shall make the trumpet to sound throughout all your land. And you shall consecrate the fiftieth year, and proclaim liberty throughout all the land to all its inhabitants. It shall be a Jubilee for you; and each of you shall return to his possession, and each of you shall return to his family. That fiftieth year shall be a Jubilee to you; in it you shall neither sow nor reap what grows of its own accord, nor gather the grapes of your untended vine."

LEVITICUS 25:1, 8–11

This teaching typifies the quietude of faith, when the full rest is reached and when the soul has no need to carry burdens or do work.

Feeding and Feasting

And if you say, "What shall we eat in the seventh year, since we shall not sow nor gather in our produce?" then I will command My blessing on you in the sixth year, and it will bring forth produce enough for three years. And you shall sow in the eighth year, and eat old produce until the ninth year; until its produce comes in, you shall eat of the old harvest.   LEVITICUS 25:20–22

Notice the question of unbelief in verse 20: "What shall we eat?" and the answer in verse 22: "You shall eat of the old harvest." The old harvest is a type of the store that is laid up for us in Christ, who "became for us wisdom...and righteousness and sanctification and redemption" (1 Corinthians 1:30).

And the sabbath produce of the land shall be food for you: for you, your male and female servants, your hired man, and the stranger who dwells with you, for your livestock and the beasts that are in your land; all its produce shall be for food.
                          LEVITICUS 25:6–7

In divine things, our "keeping of Sabbaths," or our resting in God's work on our behalf, brings to us our richest blessings. Our rest is "food" for us, and for all who belong to us. Moreover, our resting is "feasts" to the Lord.

And the LORD spoke to Moses, saying, "Speak to the children of Israel, and say to them: 'The feasts of the LORD, which you shall proclaim to be holy convocations, these are My feasts. Six days shall work be done, but the seventh day is a Sabbath of solemn rest, a holy convocation. You shall do no work on it; it is the Sabbath of the LORD in all your dwellings.'"   LEVITICUS 23:1–3

Resting So That God Can Rest

On the days of the Lord's feasts, no work was to be done. Notice the expression so frequently used in the twenty-third chapter of Leviticus: "You shall do no customary ["servile" KJV] work on it" (verses 7, 8, 21, 25, 35, 36). There are many Christians who try to keep the feasts of the Lord by doing "servile work"— that is, work that is done from duty only and not from love; work that is a great cross and a heavy burden, and that would not be done at all if the soul could hope to get to heaven by any other pathway.

> And any person who does any work on that same day, that person I will destroy from among his people. You shall do no manner of work; it shall be a statute forever throughout your generations in all your dwellings. It shall be to you a sabbath of solemn rest.   LEVITICUS 23:30–32

We cannot feast while those we love are toiling, nor can our God.

> And David said to Solomon: "My son, as for me, it was in my mind to build a house to the name of the LORD my God; but the word of the LORD came to me, saying, 'You have shed much blood and have made great wars; you shall not build a house for My name, because you have shed much blood on the earth in My sight. Behold, a son shall be born to you, who shall be a man of rest; and I will give him rest from all his enemies all around. His name shall be Solomon, for I will give peace and quietness to Israel in his days. He shall build a

house for My name, and he shall be My son, and I will be his Father; and I will establish the throne of his kingdom over Israel forever.'"

1 CHRONICLES 22:7–10

The Lord cannot make His abode in the midst of conflict and unrest, and we cannot know His abiding presence in the inward temple of our hearts while our experience is only one of conflict. An interior rest must be realized before this inward divine union can be known.

For as yet you have not come to the rest and the inheritance which the LORD your God is giving you. But when you cross over the Jordan and dwell in the land which the LORD your God is giving you to inherit, and He gives you rest from all your enemies round about, so that you dwell in safety, then there will be the place where the LORD your God chooses to make His name abide. There you shall bring all that I command you.

DEUTERONOMY 12:9–11

David also commanded all the leaders of Israel to help Solomon his son, saying, "Is not the LORD your God with you? And has He not given you rest on every side? For He has given the inhabitants of the land into my hand, and the land is subdued before the LORD and before His people. Now set your heart and your soul to seek the LORD your God. Therefore arise and build the sanctuary of the LORD God, to bring the ark of the covenant of the LORD and the holy articles of God into the house that is to be built for the name of the LORD."

1 CHRONICLES 22:17–19

The Lord rests when we rest.

Now therefore, arise, O LORD God, to Your resting place, You and the ark of Your strength. Let Your priests, O LORD God, be clothed with salvation, and let Your saints rejoice in goodness.

2 CHRONICLES 6:41

For the LORD has chosen Zion; He has desired it for His dwelling place: "This is My resting place forever; here I will dwell, for I have desired it."

PSALM 132:13–14

A mother cannot rest while her little ones are toiling or bearing burdens. She must see them all at rest before she herself can be comfortable. So it is with our God.

"Yes, Lord"

Some essentials for soul rest are expressed in the following verses:

[Jesus said,] "Come to Me, all you who labor and are heavy laden, and I will give you rest. Take My yoke upon you and learn from Me,...and you will find rest for your souls."   MATTHEW 11:28–29

We who have believed do enter that rest.

HEBREWS 4:3

Surrender, faith, and obedience are necessary at every step of the divine progress, and nowhere are they more necessary than in the matter of rest for the soul. Without them, rest is simply impossible. The little child rests in his mother's arms only when he yields unquestioning submission to her control and trusts implicitly in her love. The ox that yields to the yoke without resisting rests under it, while the young bull "unaccustomed to the yoke" (Jeremiah 31:18 KJV) finds it a galling burden. Truly, many Christians have less sense than animals. The animals, when they find the yoke inevitable, yield to it, and it becomes easy, while we are tempted to resist it and worry under it as long as life lasts.

Learn to "take" the yoke upon you. Do not wait for it to be forced on you, but bow your neck to it willingly and take it. Say "Yes, Lord" to each expression of His will in all the circumstances of your life. Say it with full consent to everything—to the loss of your money, to the loss of your health, to the malice of enemies, or to the cruelty of friends. Take each yoke as it comes, and in the taking you will find rest.

Notice the expressions in Matthew 11:28–29: "I will *give* you rest" and "You will *find* rest" (emphasis added). This rest cannot be earned or bought or attained. It is simply *given* by God and *found* by us. All who come to Christ in the way of surrender and trust, "find" it without any effort. They "enter that rest" (Hebrews 4:3).

Total Tranquillity

In God's presence, there is never any unrest.

And He said, "My Presence will go with you, and I will give you rest." EXODUS 33:14

The mere presence of the mother is perfect rest to the little babe, no matter what tumult or danger may surround him. If we only knew God, His presence would be perfect rest to us.

When He gives quietness, who then can make trouble? JOB 34:29

Among the peaks of the Sierra Nevada Mountains—just a couple hundred miles from the busy whirl of San Francisco, the great metropolis of the Pacific coast—lies Lake Tahoe. It is twenty-two miles long, twelve miles wide, and over nineteen hundred feet deep; and it lies about six thousand feet above the neighboring ocean. Storms come and go in lower waters, but all the while this lake is so still and its water so clear that the eye can penetrate, it is said, a hundred feet into its depths. In this region, a bell can be heard for ten or twenty miles. Around the lake's green edges are the mountains, ever crowned with snow. The sky above is as calm as the motionless water. Nature scarcely loses anything of its clear outline as it is reflected in the crystal water. Here the soul may learn something of what rest is, as day after day one opens his heart to let the sweet influences of nature's Sabbath enter and reign. And this rest is but a faint taste of what we may find in Christ.

In the pressure of the greatest responsibilities, in the worry of the smallest cares, in the perplexity of life's moments of crisis, we may have the Lake Tahoe rest in the hidden retreats of God's will. Learn to live in this rest. In the calmness of spirit that it will give, your soul will reflect, like in a mirror, "the beauty of the LORD" (Psalm 90:17). The tumult of men's lives will be calmed in your presence, as your tumults have been calmed in the presence of God.

The work of righteousness will be peace, and the effect of righteousness, quietness and assurance forever. My people will dwell in a peaceful habitation, in secure dwellings, and in quiet resting places.   ISAIAH 32:17–18

Chapter 7

Fruit-Bearing

[Jesus said,] "You did not choose Me, but I chose you and appointed you that you should go and bear fruit, and that your fruit should remain, that whatever you ask the Father in My name He may give you."
—John 15:16

God saved us so that we would bring forth fruit. A vinedresser plants a vine for the sake of the grapes it will bear; a farmer plants an apple orchard in order to gather fruit. A fruitless Christian life is an impossibility.

[Jesus said,] "I am the true vine, and My Father is the vinedresser. Every branch in Me that does not bear fruit He takes away; and every branch that bears fruit He prunes, that it may bear more fruit." JOHN 15:1–2

And even now the ax is laid to the root of the trees. Therefore every tree which does not bear good fruit is cut down and thrown into the fire.

LUKE 3:9

Many people have a tendency to think far more of being saved than of being fruitful. But God does not separate these two things. To be saved is to be fruitful, and to be fruitful is to be saved.

[Jesus] also spoke this parable: "A certain man had a fig tree planted in his vineyard, and he came seeking fruit on it and found none. Then he said to the keeper of his vineyard, 'Look, for three years I have come seeking fruit on this fig tree and find none. Cut it down; why does it use up the ground?' But he answered and said to him, 'Sir, let it alone this year also, until I dig around it and fertilize it. And if it bears fruit, well. But if not, after that you can cut it down.'"   LUKE 13:6–9

For the earth which drinks in the rain that often comes upon it, and bears herbs useful for those by whom it is cultivated, receives blessing from God; but if it bears thorns and briars, it is rejected and near to being cursed, whose end is to be burned.
                              HEBREWS 6:7–8

TO BE OR TO DO

No matter how good our lives may appear to be outwardly, no matter how clear our doctrines or how great our activities, unless we bear fruit we cannot be acceptable to God. The fruit He desires is character. He wants us to be right with Him even more than He wants us to do right. Of course, the doing will follow the being, but the vital point is the being.

Most people have reversed this order and have made the doing the vital thing, limiting the meaning

of fruit-bearing to service—so much work done, so
many meetings held, so many sermons preached, so
many prayers prayed, so many results accomplished.
But God's primary idea of fruit is Christlikeness.

But the fruit of the Spirit is love, joy, peace, longsuffering, kindness, goodness, faithfulness, gentleness, self-control. Against such there is no law.
GALATIANS 5:22–23

For the fruit of the Spirit is in all goodness, righteousness, and truth. EPHESIANS 5:9

For whom He foreknew, He also predestined to be
conformed to the image of His Son, that He might
be the firstborn among many brethren.
ROMANS 8:29

And this I pray, that your love may abound still
more and more in knowledge and all discernment,
that you may approve the things that are excellent, that you may be sincere and without offense
till the day of Christ, being filled with the fruits of
righteousness which are by Jesus Christ, to the
glory and praise of God. PHILIPPIANS 1:9–11

People may do much wonderful so-called Christian work yet, in it all, fail to bear one single fruit of
righteousness that will be "to the glory and praise of
God."

But the wisdom that is from above is first pure,
then peaceable, gentle, willing to yield, full of
mercy and good fruits, without partiality and

without hypocrisy. Now the fruit of righteousness is sown in peace by those who make peace.

JAMES 3:17–18

[Jesus said,] "You will know them by their fruits. Do men gather grapes from thornbushes or figs from thistles? Even so, every good tree bears good fruit, but a bad tree bears bad fruit. A good tree cannot bear bad fruit, nor can a bad tree bear good fruit. Every tree that does not bear good fruit is cut down and thrown into the fire. Therefore by their fruits you will know them."

MATTHEW 7:16–20

Some Christians have what is sometimes called a "public gift," meaning that they can speak or pray in a church service to great edification. However, some of these same people go home and are quick-tempered with their families, bitter toward their acquaintances, faultfinding, malicious, and full of self. They appear to have great outward results during church services, but they do not yet have the very first and most vital aspect of the fruit of the Spirit, which is love. Consequently, everything else, grand as it may seem, "profits [them] nothing."

Though I speak with the tongues of men and of angels, but have not love, I have become sounding brass or a clanging cymbal. And though I have the gift of prophecy, and understand all mysteries and all knowledge, and though I have all faith, so that I could remove mountains, but have not love, I am nothing. And though I bestow all my goods to feed the poor, and though I give my body to be burned, but have not love, it profits me nothing.

1 CORINTHIANS 13:1–3

SELF-CENTERED SERVICE

Israel empties his vine; he brings forth fruit for himself. According to the multitude of his fruit he has increased the altars [to heathen gods]; according to the bounty of his land they have embellished his sacred pillars [idols]. HOSEA 10:1

"Brings forth fruit for himself" means simply that self is the center and the end of all the work. To bring glory to self, to gain advantage for self, to secure future rewards for self, to exalt self in some way—this is the secret aim of such service, and God calls it an empty vine.

[Jesus said,] "Either make the tree good and its fruit good, or else make the tree bad and its fruit bad; for a tree is known by its fruit. Brood of vipers! How can you, being evil, speak good things? For out of the abundance of the heart the mouth speaks. A good man out of the good treasure of his heart brings forth good things, and an evil man out of the evil treasure brings forth evil things." MATTHEW 12:33–35

There is no possible way for "an evil man" to bring forth good things. It is an unavoidable fact, even if he does not know it and surely does not intend to live by it, that "out of the abundance of the heart" the life will be lived. In spiritual matters, we cannot pretend. If our tree is corrupt, our fruit will be corrupt also, no matter how much we may try to fix it up or make it appear good.

[Jesus said,] "For a good tree does not bear bad fruit, nor does a bad tree bear good fruit. For every tree is known by its own fruit. For men do not gather figs from thorns, nor do they gather grapes from a bramble bush. A good man out of the good treasure of his heart brings forth good; and an evil man out of the evil treasure of his heart brings forth evil. For out of the abundance of the heart his mouth speaks."   LUKE 6:43–45

If the fruit of the Spirit—which is love, longsuffering, kindness, gentleness, and so on—is not seen in a person's life, then the Spirit cannot be there either; for where the Spirit is, His fruit must of necessity be manifest.

But when he [John the Baptist] saw many of the Pharisees and Sadducees coming to his baptism, he said to them, "Brood of vipers! Who warned you to flee from the wrath to come? Therefore bear fruits worthy of repentance, and do not think to say to yourselves, 'We have Abraham as our father.' For I say to you that God is able to raise up children to Abraham from these stones. And even now the ax is laid to the root of the trees. Therefore every tree which does not bear good fruit is cut down and thrown into the fire."
                MATTHEW 3:7–10

Even to have "Abraham as our father" will not save us, nor will any other outward relationship or position. The fruit of the Spirit can come only from the Spirit; and without this fruit, no one can claim to be walking in the Spirit, no matter what his outward activities or position in the church may be.

Because they hated knowledge and did not choose the fear of the LORD, they would have none of my

counsel and despised my every rebuke. Therefore they shall eat the fruit of their own way, and be filled to the full with their own fancies.
PROVERBS 1:29–31

"The fruit of [our] own way" may look appealing to the eye of flesh, but the soul that is compelled to eat it will find itself starved in regard to its true inner life.

I, the LORD, search the heart, I test the mind, even to give every man according to his ways, according to the fruit of his doings.   JEREMIAH 17:10

Man may judge by outward appearances (1 Samuel 16:7), but the Lord searches the heart and gives to each one of us according to the fruit He finds there.

Christian workers especially need to realize this truth. They need to understand that no amount of preaching, praying, singing, weeping, or groaning can take the place of being gentle, meek, longsuffering, and good.

A multitude of people want to work for the Lord but do not want to be good for Him. However, it is the goodness that He cares for, far more than the work. If you cannot do both, choose to be good, for it is infinitely more important.

Now let me sing to my Well-beloved a song of my Beloved regarding His vineyard: My Well-beloved has a vineyard on a very fruitful hill. He dug it up and cleared out its stones, and planted it with the choicest vine. He built a tower in its midst, and also made a winepress in it; so He expected it to bring forth good grapes, but it brought forth wild grapes. "And now, O inhabitants of Jerusalem and men of Judah, judge, please, between Me and My vineyard. What more could have been done to My vineyard that I have not done in it? Why then, when I expected it to bring forth good grapes, did it bring forth wild grapes? And now, please let Me tell you what I will do to My vineyard: I will take away its hedge, and it shall be burned; and break down its wall, and it shall be trampled down. I will lay it waste; it shall not be pruned or dug, but there shall come up briers and thorns. I will also command the clouds that they rain no rain on it." For the vineyard of the LORD of hosts is the house of Israel, and the men of Judah are His pleasant plant. He looked for justice, but behold, oppression; for righteousness, but behold, a cry for help.

ISAIAH 5:1–7

We must see to it that the fruit we bring forth in our lives does not have the nature of "wild grapes," which sicken all with whom we live. Unfortunately, there are too many such people to be found, sometimes even among those who are so-called pillars in the church. If their families could speak, they would tell of "oppression" and "a cry" that would wring our hearts because of its pitiful sadness.

For their vine is of the vine of Sodom and of the fields of Gomorrah; their grapes are grapes of gall, their clusters are bitter. DEUTERONOMY 32:32

Yet I had planted you a noble vine, a seed of highest quality. How then have you turned before Me into the degenerate plant of an alien vine? JEREMIAH 2:21

GOOD FRUIT GROWS IN A GOOD HEART

How, then, does this good fruit come? There is only one way in which it can come. It grows from the seed that God plants.

And He said, "The kingdom of God is as if a man should scatter seed on the ground, and should sleep by night and rise by day, and the seed should sprout and grow, he himself does not know how. For the earth yields crops by itself: first the blade, then the head, after that the full grain in the head. But when the grain ripens, immediately he puts in the sickle, because the harvest has come." Then He said, "To what shall we liken the kingdom of God? Or with what parable shall we picture it? It is like a mustard seed which, when it is sown on the ground, is smaller than all the seeds on earth; but when it is sown, it grows up and becomes greater than all herbs, and shoots out large branches, so that the birds of the air may nest under its shade." MARK 4:26–32

Then He taught them many things by parables, and said to them in His teaching: "Listen! Behold, a sower went out to sow. And it happened, as he sowed, that some seed fell by the wayside; and the birds of the air came and devoured it. Some fell on stony ground, where it did not have much earth; and immediately it sprang up because it had no depth of earth. But when the sun was up it was scorched, and because it had no root it withered away. And some seed fell among thorns; and the thorns grew up and choked it, and it yielded no crop. But other seed fell on good ground and

yielded a crop that sprang up, increased and produced: some thirtyfold, some sixty, and some a
hundred." MARK 4:2–8

Fruit does not come by effort, but by growth. It
unfolds from within. There must first be a good inward life before there can be good outward fruit. As I
asked in an earlier chapter, what would we think of
a farmer who tried to make an orchard by beginning
with the apples? Suppose he collected bushel after
bushel of excellent apples, tied them onto branches,
fastened the branches onto tree trunks, then fastened the tree trunks onto the roots, and finally
planted the manufactured trees in the ground. We
would look upon his efforts as madness. Yet this
would not be more foolish than trying to begin the
Christian life with works instead of with character.

[Jesus said,] "Which of you by worrying can add
one cubit to his stature? So why do you worry
about clothing? Consider the lilies of the field, how
they grow: they neither toil nor spin; and yet I say
to you that even Solomon in all his glory was not
arrayed like one of these. Now if God so clothes
the grass of the field, which today is, and tomorrow is thrown into the oven, will He not much
more clothe you, O you of little faith?"
 MATTHEW 6:27–30

[Jesus said,] "A good tree cannot bear bad fruit,
nor can a bad tree bear good fruit." MATTHEW 7:18

Notice the word "cannot" in this passage. It
does not say "will not," but "cannot." This verse

expresses an absolute impossibility. No outward pretending, therefore, will help at all in the matter of fruit-bearing. The tree itself must be good, or the fruit it bears "cannot" be good, work as hard as we may.

Some people always walk on spiritual stilts when in front of others. If they are traveling with others, they take out their Bibles in order to look pious. When they write a letter, they try to put in some expressions that will show their religion. They season their conversation with pious comments. They can never afford to be natural in the presence of others, for fear that they will not be considered as religious as they really are. They do their works to be "seen by men," and they do indeed "have their reward." Man sees and praises, but God sees and condemns.

[Jesus said,] "Take heed that you do not do your charitable deeds before men, to be seen by them. Otherwise you have no reward from your Father in heaven. Therefore, when you do a charitable deed, do not sound a trumpet before you as the hypocrites do in the synagogues and in the streets, that they may have glory from men. Assuredly, I say to you, they have their reward. But when you do a charitable deed, do not let your left hand know what your right hand is doing, that your charitable deed may be in secret; and your Father who sees in secret will Himself reward you openly. And when you pray, you shall not be like the hypocrites. For they love to pray standing in the synagogues and on the corners of the streets, that they may be seen by men. Assuredly, I say to you, they have their reward." MATTHEW 6:1–5

A man can never be more than his character makes him. A man can never do more than what his character produces. Nothing valuable can come out of a man that is not first in the man. Character must stand behind and back up everything a believer does, whether it is preaching a sermon, writing a poem, painting a picture, or authoring a book. These things are not worth one iota unless backed by character.

Out of the same mouth proceed blessing and cursing. My brethren, these things ought not to be so. Does a spring send forth fresh water and bitter from the same opening? Can a fig tree, my brethren, bear olives, or a grapevine bear figs? Thus no spring yields both salt water and fresh. Who is wise and understanding among you? Let him show by good conduct that his works are done in the meekness of wisdom. But if you have bitter envy and self-seeking in your hearts, do not boast and lie against the truth. This wisdom does not descend from above, but is earthly, sensual, demonic. For where envy and self-seeking exist, confusion and every evil thing are there. But the wisdom that is from above is first pure, then peaceable, gentle, willing to yield, full of mercy and good fruits, without partiality and without hypocrisy. Now the fruit of righteousness is sown in peace by those who make peace.   JAMES 3:10–18

So Jesus said, "Are you also still without understanding? Do you not yet understand that whatever enters the mouth goes into the stomach and is eliminated? But those things which proceed out of the mouth come from the heart, and they defile a man. For out of the heart proceed evil thoughts,

murders, adulteries, fornications, thefts, false witness, blasphemies. These are the things which defile a man, but to eat with unwashed hands does
not defile a man."   MATTHEW 15:16–20

Character, then, is the essential thing. What is
in the heart and what comes "out of the heart" are
the only realities in life. If we fail to see this fact, we
are yet, as our Lord said, "without understanding."
A fig tree cannot bear both figs and thistles;
likewise, "blessing" and "cursing" cannot be the
fruit of the same spirit.

[Jesus said,] "No one can serve two masters; for
either he will hate the one and love the other, or
else he will be loyal to the one and despise the
other. You cannot serve God and mammon."
                                        MATTHEW 6:24

For when you were slaves of sin, you were free in
regard to righteousness. What fruit did you have
then in the things of which you are now ashamed?
For the end of those things is death. But now
having been set free from sin, and having become
slaves of God, you have your fruit to holiness, and
the end, everlasting life.   ROMANS 6:20–22

THE SECRET OF A FRUIT-FILLED LIFE

What, then, is the secret of true fruit-bearing?

[Jesus said,] "Abide in Me, and I in you. As the
branch cannot bear fruit of itself, unless it abides
in the vine, neither can you, unless you abide in

Me. I am the vine, you are the branches. He who abides in Me, and I in him, bears much fruit; for without Me you can do nothing. If anyone does not abide in Me, he is cast out as a branch and is withered; and they gather them and throw them into the fire, and they are burned. If you abide in Me, and My words abide in you, you will ask what you desire, and it shall be done for you. By this My Father is glorified, that you bear much fruit; so you will be My disciples."   JOHN 15:4–8

Here, again, we have an inflexible rule: "The branch *cannot* bear fruit of itself" (emphasis added). Try as hard as we may, no fruit is possible unless we abide in Christ. Other things are possible—wonderful works, perhaps; eminent service; great benevolence—but not the fruit of the Spirit. This fruit cannot come from any other source than the indwelling Spirit.

Therefore, my brethren, you also have become dead to the law through the body of Christ, that you may be married to another; to Him who was raised from the dead, that we should bear fruit to God. For when we were in the flesh, the sinful passions which were aroused by the law were at work in our members to bear fruit to death.
                        ROMANS 7:4–5

I will be like the dew to Israel; he shall grow like the lily, and lengthen his roots like Lebanon. His branches shall spread; his beauty shall be like an olive tree, and his fragrance like Lebanon. Those who dwell under his shadow shall return; they shall be revived like grain, and grow like a vine.

Their scent shall be like the wine of Lebanon. "Ephraim shall say, 'What have I to do anymore with idols?' I have heard and observed him. I am like a green cypress tree; your fruit is found in Me."   HOSEA 14:5–8

Those who come He shall cause to take root in Jacob; Israel shall blossom and bud, and fill the face of the world with fruit.   ISAIAH 27:6

"Your fruit is found in Me," the Lord says. Not from anything of the flesh, not from our own activities, not from anything of self in any way, but from God alone. He alone can perfect His own fruit.

GROWING PAINS

[Jesus said,] "Every branch in Me that does not bear fruit He takes away; and every branch that bears fruit He prunes, that it may bear more fruit."   JOHN 15:2

It is the vinedresser's business to prune and purge the vine in order to make it fruitful. Accordingly, we must accept all the storms and sorrows of life as the purgings necessary to make us bring forth "more fruit." To an inexperienced onlooker, the trimming and cutting of the vinedresser often seem ruthless, and he might cry out to him to spare the vine. But in the autumn, when the rich clusters of fruit are hanging from the same vine, he acknowledges the vinedresser's wisdom and applauds his skill.

Similarly, in our soul life we may be tempted to sometimes question the wisdom or the goodness of the divine Vinedresser, when He sees fit to cut off our most flourishing branches or to trim our life of its dearest joys. But the Vinedresser knows what is best for His vine, and we must leave the entire matter to Him.

> For our light affliction, which is but for a moment, is working for us a far more exceeding and eternal weight of glory. 2 CORINTHIANS 4:17

> And you have forgotten the exhortation which speaks to you as to sons: "My son, do not despise the chastening of the LORD, nor be discouraged when you are rebuked by Him; for whom the LORD loves He chastens, and scourges every son whom He receives." If you endure chastening, God deals with you as with sons; for what son is there whom a father does not chasten? But if you are without chastening, of which all have become partakers, then you are illegitimate and not sons. Furthermore, we have had human fathers who corrected us, and we paid them respect. Shall we not much more readily be in subjection to the Father of spirits and live? For they indeed for a few days chastened us as seemed best to them, but He for our profit, that we may be partakers of His holiness. Now no chastening seems to be joyful for the present, but painful; nevertheless, afterward it yields the peaceable fruit of righteousness to those who have been trained by it. HEBREWS 12:5–11

FOUR STEPS TO A FRUITFUL FUTURE

What, then, must we do if we want to bring forth "much fruit" (John 15:5)?

First, we must abandon ourselves to the Lord and trust Him perfectly.

Blessed is the man who trusts in the LORD, and whose hope is the LORD. For he shall be like a tree planted by the waters, which spreads out its roots by the river, and will not fear when heat comes; but its leaf will be green, and will not be anxious in the year of drought, nor will cease from yielding fruit.   JEREMIAH 17:7–8

Blessed is the man who walks not in the counsel of the ungodly, nor stands in the path of sinners, nor sits in the seat of the scornful; but his delight is in the law of the LORD, and in His law he meditates day and night. He shall be like a tree planted by the rivers of water, that brings forth its fruit in its season, whose leaf also shall not wither; and whatever he does shall prosper. The ungodly are not so, but are like the chaff which the wind drives away.
                                                    PSALM 1:1–4

Second, we must receive the truth and believe it, and we must keep on steadfastly believing it, no matter how things may appear.

[Jesus said,] "Now the parable is this: The seed is the word of God. Those by the wayside are the ones who hear; then the devil comes and takes away the word out of their hearts, lest they should believe and be saved. But the ones on the rock are those who, when they hear, receive the word with joy; and these have no root, who believe for a while and in time of temptation fall away. Now the ones that fell among thorns are those who, when they have heard, go out and are choked with cares, riches, and pleasures of life, and bring no fruit to maturity. But the ones that fell on the good ground are those who, having heard the word with a noble and good heart, keep it and bear fruit with patience." LUKE 8:11–15

Then it shall come to pass, because you listen to these judgments, and keep and do them, that the LORD your God will keep with you the covenant and the mercy which He swore to your fathers. And He will love you and bless you and multiply you; He will also bless the fruit of your womb and the fruit of your land, your grain and your new wine and your oil, the increase of your cattle and the offspring of your flock, in the land of which He swore to your fathers to give you. You shall be blessed above all peoples; there shall not be a male or female barren among you or among your livestock. DEUTERONOMY 7:12–14

But if you do not obey Me, and do not observe all these commandments, and if you despise My statutes, or if your soul abhors My judgments, so that you do not perform all My commandments, but break My covenant,...your strength shall be spent in vain; for your land shall not yield its produce, nor shall the trees of the land yield their fruit. LEVITICUS 26:14–15, 20

Third, we must submit ourselves to God's will and obey His voice.

If you walk in My statutes and keep My commandments, and perform them, then I will give

131

you rain in its season, the land shall yield its produce, and the trees of the field shall yield their fruit. Your threshing shall last till the time of vintage, and the vintage shall last till the time of sowing; you shall eat your bread to the full, and dwell in your land safely.   LEVITICUS 26:3–5

And all these blessings shall come upon you and overtake you, because you obey the voice of the LORD your God: Blessed shall you be in the city, and blessed shall you be in the country. Blessed shall be the fruit of your body, the produce of your ground and the increase of your herds, the increase of your cattle and the offspring of your flocks. Blessed shall be your basket and your kneading bowl....And the LORD will grant you plenty of goods, in the fruit of your body, in the increase of your livestock, and in the produce of your ground, in the land of which the LORD swore to your fathers to give you.   DEUTERONOMY 28:2–5, 11

Fourth, we must die to the self-life and must be alive only to the indwelling life of Christ.

[Jesus said,] "Most assuredly, I say to you, unless a grain of wheat falls into the ground and dies, it remains alone; but if it dies, it produces much grain. He who loves his life will lose it, and he who hates his life in this world will keep it for eternal life."   JOHN 12:24–25

[Christ] Himself bore our sins in His own body on the tree, that we, having died to sins, might live for righteousness; by whose stripes you were healed.   1 PETER 2:24

For when we were in the flesh, the sinful passions which were aroused by the law were at work in our members to bear fruit to death. But now we have been delivered from the law, having died to what we were held by, so that we should serve in the newness of the Spirit and not in the oldness of the letter.   ROMANS 7:5–6

Again, in order to bring forth the fruit of the Spirit, we must "live in the Spirit," and we must die to all that is of the flesh. If we want to bear fruit unto God, we must stop bearing fruit unto self.

And those who are Christ's have crucified the flesh with its passions and desires. If we live in the Spirit, let us also walk in the Spirit.
                                    GALATIANS 5:24–25

Put off, concerning your former conduct, the old man which grows corrupt according to the deceitful lusts, and be renewed in the spirit of your mind, and...put on the new man which was created according to God, in true righteousness and holiness.   EPHESIANS 4:22–24

Is Your Life a Blessing to Others?

While the primary sense of fruit-bearing is character, there is also a fruitfulness in service that follows as the outcome of this inward life. Since fruit always springs from seeds, growth will invariably follow the blossoming stage. The fruit is simply the wrapping that is around the seed.

If your fruit-bearing is real and not fake, your life will sow seeds in the world around you that will spring up in wondrous fruitfulness in the hearts of others.

For this reason we also, since the day we heard it, do not cease to pray for you, and to ask that you may be filled with the knowledge of His will in all wisdom and spiritual understanding; that you may walk worthy of the Lord, fully pleasing Him, being fruitful in every good work and increasing in the knowledge of God.   COLOSSIANS 1:9–10

Therefore by Him let us continually offer the sacrifice of praise to God, that is, the fruit of our lips, giving thanks to His name.   HEBREWS 13:15

I will make them and the places all around My hill a blessing; and I will cause showers to come down in their season; there shall be showers of blessing. Then the trees of the field shall yield their fruit, and the earth shall yield her increase. They shall be safe in their land; and they shall know that I am the LORD.   EZEKIEL 34:26–27

For the seed shall be prosperous, the vine shall give its fruit, the ground shall give her increase, and the heavens shall give their dew; I will cause the remnant of this people to possess all these. And it shall come to pass that just as you were a curse among the nations, O house of Judah and house of Israel, so I will save you, and you shall be a blessing. Do not fear, let your hands be strong.   ZECHARIAH 8:12–13

Does your fruit cover a seed of good? Are you a blessing? Is there so much sweetness, gentleness, meekness, and love in your daily existence that you sow seeds of blessing in the hearts of your family, friends, and neighbors? Or does your life sow seeds of hatred, anger, and all unlovely and un-Christlike things?

> Do not be deceived, God is not mocked; for whatever a man sows, that he will also reap. For he who sows to his flesh will of the flesh reap corruption, but he who sows to the Spirit will of the Spirit reap everlasting life. And let us not grow weary while doing good, for in due season we shall reap if we do not lose heart.   GALATIANS 6:7–9

There is no more solemn fact in all the universe than this: what a man sows he will also reap. The only way to escape this harvest is to root out the seed that has been sown to the flesh and to plant a new crop. We must begin to bring forth fruit unto God and from God only, that is, the divine fruit of the Spirit, whose seed will spring up in blessing for everyone around us.

> [Jesus said,] "Let your light so shine before men, that they may see your good works and glorify your Father in heaven."   MATTHEW 5:16

> For you were bought at a price; therefore glorify God in your body and in your spirit, which are God's.   1 CORINTHIANS 6:20

> Clearly you are an epistle of Christ, ministered by us, written not with ink but by the Spirit of the living God, not on tablets of stone but on tablets of flesh, that is, of the heart.   2 CORINTHIANS 3:3

WILL GOD FIND FRUIT IN YOUR LIFE?

It may well be that our divine Vinedresser is seeking fruit at this very moment from many of the vines that He has planted but is finding none, in spite of a great outward show of greenness and vigor.

Now the next day, when they had come out from Bethany, He was hungry. And seeing from afar a fig tree having leaves, He went to see if perhaps He would find something on it. When He came to it, He found nothing but leaves, for it was not the season for figs.   MARK 11:12–13

These are spots in your love feasts, while they feast with you without fear, serving only themselves. They are clouds without water, carried about by the winds; late autumn trees without fruit, twice dead, pulled up by the roots.   JUDE 12

They [the chief priests and the elders] said to Him, "He will destroy those wicked men miserably, and lease his vineyard to other vinedressers who will render to him the fruits in their seasons." Jesus said to them, "Have you never read in the Scriptures: 'The stone which the builders rejected has become the chief cornerstone. This was the Lord's doing, and it is marvelous in our eyes'? Therefore I say to you, the kingdom of God will be taken from you and given to a nation bearing the fruits of it."
                    MATTHEW 21:41–43

Let us be among the number of those whose fruit is so truly the fruit of the Spirit that it is always to the praise of God's glory.

A garden enclosed is my sister, my spouse, a spring shut up, a fountain sealed. Your plants are an orchard of pomegranates with pleasant fruits, fragrant henna with spikenard, spikenard and saffron, calamus and cinnamon, with all trees of frankincense, myrrh and aloes, with all the chief spices; a fountain of gardens, a well of living waters, and streams from Lebanon.   SONG OF SOLOMON 4:12–15

The righteous shall flourish like a palm tree, he shall grow like a cedar in Lebanon. Those who are planted in the house of the LORD shall flourish in the courts of our God. They shall still bear fruit in old age; they shall be fresh and flourishing.
PSALM 92:12–14

Let us be content with whatever purging or pruning our divine Vinedresser may deem necessary for our perfecting, eager only to store up "pleasant fruits" (Song of Solomon 4:16) for our Beloved, so that He may "see the labor of His soul, and be satisfied" (Isaiah 53:11).

Awake, O north wind, and come, O south! Blow upon my garden, that its spices may flow out. Let my beloved come to his garden and eat its pleasant fruits.   SONG OF SOLOMON 4:16

I have come to my garden, my sister, my spouse; I have gathered my myrrh with my spice; I have eaten my honeycomb with my honey; I have drunk my wine with my milk....Eat, O friends! Drink, yes, drink deeply, O beloved ones!
SONG OF SOLOMON 5:1

The mandrakes give off a fragrance, and at our gates are pleasant fruits, all manner, new and old, which I have laid up for you, my beloved.

SONG OF SOLOMON 7:13

Chapter 8

Be Anxious for Nothing

Be anxious for nothing, but in everything by prayer and supplication, with thanksgiving, let your requests be made known to God; and the peace of God, which surpasses all understanding, will guard your hearts and minds through Christ Jesus.
—Philippians 4:6–7

Notice the word "nothing." It covers all possible grounds for anxiety, both inward and outward. We are continually tempted to believe that it is our duty to be anxious about some things. Perhaps we think, "Oh yes, it is quite right to give up all anxiety in a general way. In spiritual matters, of course, anxiety is wrong. But there *are* things about which it would be a sin not to be anxious—about our children, for instance, or those we love; about our church affairs and the cause of truth; or about our business matters. We would be hard-hearted not to be anxious about such things as these."

Or our thoughts go in a completely different direction, and we say to ourselves, "Yes, it is quite right to commit our loved ones and all our outward circumstances to the Lord. But when it comes to our inward lives—our religious experiences, our temptations, our besetting sins, our growth in grace, and all such things—these we ought to be anxious about. If we are not, they will surely be neglected."

To such and to all similar ideas, the answer is found in our text: "Be anxious for *nothing*" (emphasis added).

There is absolutely no getting away from this truth by twisting God's words. Our circumstances may seem to call for anxiety, but God knows our plight. Since He says "nothing," that settles the matter forever.

A BIBLE LESSON FROM A BIRD

Our Lord showed us the reason that we are not to be anxious in the Sermon on the Mount:

> Therefore I say to you, do not worry about your life, what you will eat or what you will drink; nor about your body, what you will put on. Is not life more than food and the body more than clothing? Look at the birds of the air, for they neither sow nor reap nor gather into barns; yet your heavenly Father feeds them. Are you not of more value than they? Which of you by worrying can add one cubit to his stature? So why do you worry about clothing? Consider the lilies of the field, how they grow: they neither toil nor spin; and yet I say to you that even Solomon in all his glory was not arrayed like one of these. Now if God so clothes the grass of the field, which today is, and tomorrow is thrown into

the oven, will He not much more clothe you, O you of little faith? Therefore do not worry, saying, "What shall we eat?" or "What shall we drink?" or "What shall we wear?" For after all these things the Gentiles seek. For your heavenly Father knows that you need all these things. But seek first the kingdom of God and His righteousness, and all these things shall be added to you. Therefore do not worry about tomorrow, for tomorrow will worry about its own things. Sufficient for the day is its own trouble. MATTHEW 6:25–34

We cannot misunderstand the illustrations that Jesus used here. The birds and the flowers are before us continually, as living examples of what real trust is. With them, of course, it is an unconscious trust, but with us it must be an intelligent and conscious act.

An individual who had learned this lesson wrote the following about it:

Long years ago I was in the act of kneeling down before the Lord my God, when a little bird, so light and free, came and perched near my window. It preached to me, all the while hopping from spray to spray, "Oh, gloomy man, look at me and learn something. Your God made me, and if you can conceive it, He loves me and cares for me. You study Him in great problems that oppress and perplex you, and you lose sight of one-half of His ways. Learn to see your God, not in great mysteries only, but in me also. His burden on me is light; His yoke on me is easy, for I only have to submit to Him and trust. But you make yokes and burdens for yourself that are grievous to be borne, because

141

you will neither submit nor trust. I advise you to follow my example, as your Master commanded you to do. Consider that the bird and the flower are as truly from God as you are, and that their lives are examples of something that He wants to see in you also. 'Look at the birds of the air, for they neither sow nor reap nor gather into barns; yet your heavenly Father feeds them.'"

GIVING OUR PROBLEMS TO THE LORD

Therefore humble yourselves under the mighty hand of God, that He may exalt you in due time, casting all your care upon Him, for He cares for you.   1 PETER 5:6–7

We all know the relief of laying a care or a burden on an earthly friend whom we trust. Just like this, only infinitely greater, is the relief that comes to the soul that has cast all its care on the Lord.

Cast your burden on the LORD, and He shall sustain you; He shall never permit the righteous to be moved.   PSALM 55:22

Most Christians act like the man who, walking along a road weighed down by a heavy burden, was invited by a kind friend to ride in his wagon. He accepted the invitation but still kept the load on his shoulders. When asked by his friend why he did not lay it down, he replied, "Oh, it is a great deal to ask you to carry me. I could not ask you to carry my burden, too!"

The One upon whom our burdens are to be laid is able to bear them, no matter how great they may be. Yet we, who often entrust vital matters to our fellowmen and feel no fear, are afraid to trust our Lord.

Strengthen the weak hands, and make firm the feeble knees. Say to those who are fearful-hearted, "Be strong, do not fear!" ISAIAH 35:3–4

"'Fear not, for I am with you; be not dismayed, for I am your God. I will strengthen you, yes, I will help you, I will uphold you with My righteous right hand.' Behold, all those who were incensed against you shall be ashamed and disgraced; they shall be as nothing, and those who strive with you shall perish. You shall seek them and not find them; those who contended with you. Those who war against you shall be as nothing, as a nonexistent thing. For I, the LORD your God, will hold your right hand, saying to you, 'Fear not, I will help you.' Fear not, you worm Jacob, you men of Israel! I will help you," says the LORD and your Redeemer, the Holy One of Israel. ISAIAH 41:10–14

Think of the blessed, fearless confidence with which children cast their cares upon their parents, and recall how the parents love to have it that way. How often a mother, when her child is tempted to be anxious about a situation, will say, "There, there, darling, do not worry. Leave it all to me, and I will take care of it. Just trust me, and do as I say, and everything will come out all right."

The only thing that a mother asks of her child is that he will yield to her care and obey her voice; then she will take charge of all the rest. It is exactly that way with us and our God.

If you are willing and obedient, you shall eat the good of the land.   ISAIAH 1:19

You [the Israelites] said [to me (Moses)]: "...You go near and hear all that the LORD our God may say, and tell us all that the LORD our God says to you, and we will hear and do it." Then the LORD heard the voice of your words when you spoke to me, and the LORD said to me: "I have heard the voice of the words of this people which they have spoken to you. They are right in all that they have spoken. Oh, that they had such a heart in them that they would fear Me and always keep all My commandments, that it might be well with them and with their children forever!"
                              DEUTERONOMY 5:24, 27–29

So they said to Jeremiah, "Let the LORD be a true and faithful witness between us, if we do not do according to everything which the LORD your God sends us by you. Whether it is pleasing or displeasing, we will obey the voice of the LORD our God to whom we send you, that it may be well with us when we obey the voice of the LORD our God."   JEREMIAH 42:5–6

No mother can make everything go right for a disobedient child, nor can God.

But My people would not heed My voice, and Israel would have none of Me. So I gave them over to their own stubborn heart, to walk in their own counsels.   PSALM 81:11–12

If we insist on carrying our own cares, managing things our own way, and walking "in [our] own counsels," sorrow and suffering cannot fail to be the result.

Trust in the LORD with all your heart, and lean not on your own understanding; in all your ways acknowledge Him, and He shall direct your paths.
                              PROVERBS 3:5–6

One time a little girl I knew brought a bag without a string to her mother to have one supplied. The mother agreed to her request, and, threading a large, blunt needle with a string, began to push it through the hem. The child had expected her mother to sew the string on at each side of the bag like a handle, and when she saw the needle and string both disappearing inside the hem, she was puzzled and distressed.

She watched a moment and then said plaintively, "I thought my mamma would put a string on my bag when she said she would." The mother looked up from her work reassuringly and said, "Do not be troubled, darling. I'm putting the string on all right." The child watched silently for a few more moments, and still no sign of the string appeared, since it was a little difficult to push it through the narrow hem. The tears began to form, and again the plaintive voice whispered, "I *thought* my mamma

145

was a good mamma and knew how to put on strings!" This time the mother saw there was a real need of comfort, and she explained more fully. "My darling," she said, "I do know how to put a string on a bag, and this is the best way. Just trust me and wait, and it will all come out all right."

The child waited, and in a few moments the string was pushed through, a knot was tied, and the bag hung triumphantly on the little arm. The child looked thoughtfully at it and then said, "Oh, I see. What happened is just like what happens with Jesus. We give Him something to do, and He doesn't seem to be doing it right, and we are just about to worry. Then we think, 'Oh, Jesus knows how'; and we just trust Him and wait, and everything comes out all right at last."

Unless the LORD builds the house, they labor in vain who build it; unless the LORD guards the city, the watchman stays awake in vain. It is vain for you to rise up early, to sit up late, to eat the bread of sorrows; for so He gives His beloved sleep.

PSALM 127:1–2

All our care is in vain unless the Lord takes the care also; and when He does take it, all our worry is a waste. If a mother sits up late and rises up early in order to bear her child's burdens, it is so that the child may rest. It would grieve her greatly to have the child try to carry the burdens as well.

THE SIN OF ANXIETY

[Jesus said,] "Let not your heart be troubled; you believe in God, believe also in Me....Peace I leave with you, My peace I give to you; not as the world gives do I give to you. Let not your heart be troubled, neither let it be afraid."   JOHN 14:1, 27

Here the Master *commanded* us not to be troubled or afraid. Every time we yield to anxiety or fear, we are disobeying Him.

There are three recorded instances in which our Lord rebuked His disciples' lack of faith, yet in each case the circumstances made anxiety seem the natural and proper thing. These events would certainly cause great worry in many Christian hearts today.

The first incident was a storm at sea.

And suddenly a great tempest arose on the sea, so that the boat was covered with the waves. But He was asleep. Then His disciples came to Him and awoke Him, saying, "Lord, save us! We are perishing!" But He said to them, "Why are you fearful, O you of little faith?" Then He arose and rebuked the winds and the sea, and there was a great calm.   MATTHEW 8:24–26

Even though the disciples' fear led them to cry to Jesus, He rebuked their fear. They ought to have known that, with Jesus aboard, they could not be anything but safe. They should have rested in quiet confidence during the storm.

The second instance was when Peter found himself sinking in the waters.

Now in the fourth watch of the night Jesus went to them, walking on the sea....And Peter...said, "Lord, if it is You, command me to come to You on

the water." So He said, "Come." And when Peter
had come down out of the boat, he walked on the
water to go to Jesus. But when he saw that the
wind was boisterous, he was afraid; and beginning
to sink he cried out, saying, "Lord, save me!" And
immediately Jesus stretched out His hand and
caught him, and said to him, "O you of little faith,
why did you doubt?"   MATTHEW 14:25, 28–31

The third occasion was when the disciples were
troubled because they had no bread.

But Jesus, being aware of it, said to them, "O you
of little faith, why do you reason among yourselves
because you have brought no bread? Do you not
yet understand, or remember the five loaves of the
five thousand and how many baskets you took up?
Nor the seven loaves of the four thousand and how
many large baskets you took up?"
                                    MATTHEW 16:8–10

Here Jesus referred them to past experiences, in
which He had supplied all their needs, as a reason
for them to trust Him in this new situation.

I am sure that Jesus was grieved at the doubts
of His disciples, just as we are grieved when those
whom we love and are trying to serve are anxious
and fearful about the things we have undertaken to
do for them.

THREE EYE-OPENING EXPERIENCES

Three instances from the Old Testament will
illustrate our lesson. The cause for anxiety in each of

these cases was very great, but in each instance God was behind the scene with His perfect supply. Those who were afraid needed only to have their eyes opened to see God's provision and to be delivered from all their fears.

The first is the story of Hagar, who was sent out from her home into the wilderness, apparently to die.

So Abraham rose early in the morning, and took bread and a skin of water; and putting it on her shoulder, he gave it and the boy to Hagar, and sent her away. Then she departed and wandered in the Wilderness of Beersheba. And the water in the skin was used up, and she placed the boy under one of the shrubs. Then she went and sat down across from him at a distance of about a bowshot; for she said to herself, "Let me not see the death of the boy." So she sat opposite him, and lifted her voice and wept. And God heard the voice of the lad. Then the angel of God called to Hagar out of heaven, and said to her, "What ails you, Hagar? Fear not, for God has heard the voice of the lad where he is. Arise, lift up the lad and hold him with your hand, for I will make him a great nation." Then God opened her eyes, and she saw a well of water. And she went and filled the skin with water, and gave the lad a drink.

GENESIS 21:14–19

The second instance was when Elijah went, during the time of famine, to the house of the widow.

So he [Elijah] arose and went to Zarephath. And when he came to the gate of the city, indeed a widow was there gathering sticks. And he called to her and said, "Please bring me a little water in a cup, that I may drink." And as she was going to get it, he called to her and said, "Please bring me a morsel of bread in your hand." So she said, "As the LORD your God lives, I do not have bread, only a handful of flour in a bin, and a little oil in a jar; and see, I am gathering a couple of sticks that I may go in and prepare it for myself and my son, that we may eat it, and die." And Elijah said to her, "Do not fear; go and do as you have said, but make me a small cake from it first, and bring it to me; and afterward make some for yourself and your son. For thus says the LORD God of Israel: 'The bin of flour shall not be used up, nor shall the jar of oil run dry, until the day the LORD sends rain on the earth.'" So she went away and did according to the word of Elijah; and she and he and her household ate for many days. The bin of flour was not used up, nor did the jar of oil run dry, according to the word of the LORD which He spoke by Elijah.   1 KINGS 17:10–16

The third time was when the army of Syria surrounded the city where Elisha was.

And when the servant of the man of God [Elisha] arose early and went out, there was an army, surrounding the city with horses and chariots. And his servant said to him, "Alas, my master! What shall we do?" So he answered, "Do not fear, for those who are with us are more than those who are with them." And Elisha prayed, and said, "LORD, I pray, open his eyes that he may see." Then the LORD opened the eyes of the young man, and he saw. And behold, the mountain was full of horses and chariots of fire all around Elisha.

2 KINGS 6:15–17

OUR TO-DO LIST

What, then, is our part in this matter?

Trust in the LORD, and do good; dwell in the land, and feed on His faithfulness. Delight yourself also in the LORD, and He shall give you the desires of your heart. Commit your way to the LORD, trust also in Him, and He shall bring it to pass. He shall bring forth your righteousness as the light, and your justice as the noonday. Rest in the LORD, and wait patiently for Him; do not fret because of him who prospers in his way, because of the man who brings wicked schemes to pass. PSALM 37:3–7

At least seven things are mentioned here: (1) Trust in the Lord, (2) Do good, (3) Delight yourself in Him, (4) Commit your way to Him, (5) Rest in Him, (6) Wait patiently for Him, and finally, (7) Do not fret.

[Jesus said,] "Therefore do not worry, saying, 'What shall we eat?' or 'What shall we drink?' or 'What shall we wear?' For after all these things the Gentiles seek. For your heavenly Father knows that you need all these things. But seek first the kingdom of God and His righteousness, and all these things shall be added to you."

MATTHEW 6:31–33

Our part, then, is to "seek first the kingdom of God and His righteousness." That is, we must make

151

it the first objective of our lives to accept His will, to do it under all circumstances, and then simply to trust Him for all the rest. In the nature of things, a person who is not fully surrendered to the Lord cannot obey His command to "be anxious for nothing" (Philippians 4:6). For unless we are satisfied with His will, we cannot trust Him to manage our lives for us.

Oh, that My people would listen to Me, that Israel would walk in My ways! I would soon subdue their enemies, and turn My hand against their adversaries....[I] would have fed them also with the finest of wheat; and with honey from the rock I would have satisfied you.   PSALM 81:13–14, 16

There is no way, therefore, but the way of full surrender and simple childlike obedience. The Lord knows what is best; we do not. Therefore, we must leave all the arrangements to Him and say about everything, "Your will be done" (Matthew 6:10).

SHOULD WE QUESTION GOD?

Remember that all questioning has the nature of doubt. In the Bible, it is called "[speaking] against God."

Yes, they spoke against God: they said, "Can God prepare a table in the wilderness? Behold, He struck the rock, so that the waters gushed out, and the streams overflowed. Can He give bread also? Can He provide meat for His people?" Therefore the LORD heard this and was furious; so a fire was kindled against Jacob, and anger also came up against Israel, because they did not believe in God, and did not trust in His salvation. Yet He had commanded the clouds above, and opened the doors of heaven, had rained down manna on them to eat, and given them of the bread of heaven.

PSALM 78:19–24

Sorrows came upon the Israelites because they did not trust. God was equal to the emergency, but they did not believe that He was, and their doubt grieved Him more than all their other sins.

So he called the name of the place Massah [Tempted] and Meribah [Contention], because of the contention of the children of Israel, and because they tempted the LORD, saying, "Is the LORD among us or not?"   EXODUS 17:7

Here their questioning is called "tempt[ing] the LORD." Yet how common is this sort of questioning among Christians, who little dream what a sin it is!

Let our Lord's own words close our lesson.

Are not five sparrows sold for two copper coins? And not one of them is forgotten before God. But the very hairs of your head are all numbered. Do not fear therefore; you are of more value than many sparrows.   LUKE 12:6–7

In the face of such assurance, who could doubt? The sparrows, and the hairs of our heads, are two strikingly insignificant and valueless things, yet they are noticed and cared for. Therefore, God surely cares for us!

The Sparrow and the Child of God

I am only a tiny sparrow,
  A bird of low degree;
My life is of little value,
  But the dear Lord cares for me.

I have no barn nor storehouse,
  I neither sow nor reap;
God gives me a sparrow's portion,
  But never a seed to keep.

I know there are many sparrows,
  All over the world they are found,
But our heavenly Father knoweth
  When one of us falls to the ground.

Tho' small, we are never forgotten,
  Tho' weak, we are never afraid;
For we know the dear Lord keepeth
  The life of the creatures He made.

I fly through the thickest forest,
  I light on many a spray;
I have no chart nor compass,
  But I never lose my way.

And I fold my wings at twilight
  Wherever I happen to be,
For the Father is always watching,
  And no harm will come to me.
I am only a little sparrow,
  A bird of low degree,
But I know the Father loves me;
  Have you less faith than we?

Chapter 9

As a Mother Comforts

As one whom his mother comforts, so I will comfort you;
and you shall be comforted in Jerusalem.
—Isaiah 66:13

We all know how a mother comforts her children, and most of us have tasted the sweetness of this comforting. Notice, then, the "as" and "so" in the verse above, and accept the divine Comforter and the heavenly comfort He offers.

> Sing, O heavens! Be joyful, O earth! And break out in singing, O mountains! For the LORD has comforted His people, and will have mercy on His afflicted. ISAIAH 49:13

> I, even I, am He who comforts you. Who are you that you should be afraid of a man who will die, and of the son of a man who will be made like grass? ISAIAH 51:12

> For the LORD will comfort Zion, He will comfort all her waste places; He will make her wilderness like

155

Eden, and her desert like the garden of the LORD; joy and gladness will be found in it, thanksgiving and the voice of melody.   ISAIAH 51:3

Break forth into joy, sing together, you waste places of Jerusalem! For the LORD has comforted His people, He has redeemed Jerusalem.

ISAIAH 52:9

God is called the "God of all comfort."

Blessed be the God and Father of our Lord Jesus Christ, the Father of mercies and God of all comfort, who comforts us in all our tribulation, that we may be able to comfort those who are in any trouble, with the comfort with which we ourselves are comforted by God.   2 CORINTHIANS 1:3–4

The Holy Spirit is called the "Comforter."

[Jesus said,] "But the Helper ["Comforter" KJV], the Holy Spirit, whom the Father will send in My name, He will teach you all things, and bring to your remembrance all things that I said to you."

JOHN 14:26

Christ, when He was leaving His disciples, made provision so that they would be comforted after He was gone.

[Jesus said,] "And I will pray the Father, and He will give you another Helper ["Comforter" KJV], that He may abide with you forever....I will not leave you orphans; I will come to you."

JOHN 14:16, 18

Some people ask, "If God is like a mother, if He comforts as a mother comforts, why is it that many people are not comforted?"

Have you ever seen a little child sitting stiff in his mother's lap and refusing to be comforted in spite of all her coaxing? Do we not often act very much the same way?

O Jerusalem, Jerusalem, the one who kills the prophets and stones those who are sent to her! How often I wanted to gather your children together, as a hen gathers her chicks under her wings, but you were not willing!   MATTHEW 23:37

In the day of my trouble I sought the Lord; my hand was stretched out in the night without ceasing; my soul refused to be comforted.   PSALM 77:2

Even a mother's love and tenderness cannot comfort a child who "refuse[s] to be comforted," nor can God's. But no sorrow can be too great for His comfort to reach, if we will only take it.

Yea, though I walk through the valley of the shadow of death, I will fear no evil; for You are with me; Your rod and Your staff, they comfort me.   PSALM 23:4

Then shall the virgin rejoice in the dance, and the young men and the old, together; for I will turn their mourning to joy, will comfort them, and make them rejoice rather than sorrow.
                                        JEREMIAH 31:13

If we will only listen believingly to Jesus' loving words, "Daughter, be of good comfort" (Matthew 9:22 KJV), we will surely be comforted.

There are many other ways in which God is like a mother. A look at these points will, I trust, open our eyes to see some truths that have been hidden from our gaze.

HE RESPONDS TO OUR CRIES

The mother runs to her child when he cries. She listens to the story of his sorrows and his needs and then relieves them. God is the same way.

> Then you shall call, and the LORD will answer; you shall cry, and He will say, "Here I am."
> ISAIAH 58:9

When the child cries, "Mother, mother, where are you?" the mother never fails to respond, "Here I am." Nor does God.

> I cried to the LORD with my voice, and He heard me from His holy hill....I lay down and slept; I awoke, for the LORD sustained me.   PSALM 3:4–5

How alert is the ear of the mother to the feeblest cry of her baby in the night! Even if she is sleeping ever so soundly, she will hear the tiny cry. How comforted and quieted the little one is when he senses the mother's presence and can go to sleep in her care.

> In the day when I cried out, You answered me, and made me bold with strength in my soul.
> PSALM 138:3

I cried out to God with my voice; to God with my voice; and He gave ear to me.   PSALM 77:1

We are sometimes tempted to think that the Lord does not hear our prayers, but let the mother teach us. Could she possibly let the cry of her child go unheeded? And is the earthly mother more tender toward her children than the heavenly Father is toward His?

He gives to the beast its food, and to the young ravens that cry.   PSALM 147:9

Since He hears the cry of the ravens, will He not hear ours?

Then they cried out to the LORD in their trouble, and He delivered them out of their distresses.
     PSALM 107:6

We are tempted to think that trouble shuts God's ears. In times of prosperity, we rejoice to believe that He hears us, but when the dark days come, we moan and complain because our prayers do not seem to reach Him. Which cry catches the mother's ear the soonest, the cry of joy or the cry of sorrow? The answer is obvious. Every mother knows that the happy noises of her children in the nursery often go unnoticed, but the slightest cry of pain or trouble reaches her ear at once. Now, is a mother more alert to the suffering of her children than our God is to His?

It shall come to pass that before they call, I will answer; and while they are still speaking, I will hear.   ISAIAH 65:24

Perhaps the child hardly knows why he cries, and cannot tell in any clear way what is the matter with him. But the mother does not refuse to listen because of this. She only seeks all the more to discover the cause of the discomfort and to remedy it. Surely, God must do the same.

He who planted the ear, shall He not hear? He who formed the eye, shall He not see?   PSALM 94:9

Behold, the Lord's hand is not shortened, that it cannot save; nor His ear heavy, that it cannot hear.   ISAIAH 59:1

Let us never grieve God again by doubting that He hears us, however faint and feeble our cry may be. Moreover, let us be encouraged to ask, as children do, for everything we need. We can be sure that He will always hear and "will always answer," as someone once said, "either in kind or in kindness."

[Jesus said,] "Until now you have asked nothing in My name. Ask, and you will receive, that your joy may be full."   JOHN 16:24

HE CARRIES AND HOLDS US

The mother carries the child in her arms and holds him close to her heart.

He will feed His flock like a shepherd; He will gather the lambs with His arm, and carry them in His bosom.   ISAIAH 40:11

Even to your old age, I am He, and even to gray
hairs I will carry you! I have made, and I will bear;
even I will carry, and will deliver you.   ISAIAH 46:4

Do we not act sometimes as if we were carrying
the Lord instead of the other way around? Are we
not weighed down under this imaginary burden
when we ought to be resting peacefully in His arms?
A baby, safe in his mother's arms, will sometimes
make little clutches of fright, as though his safety
depended on the strength of his tiny grasp on the
mother. But the mother knows how useless these
movements are; she knows that it is *her* grasp, not
the baby's, that secures his safety. Surely this is true
of our security in the arms of God.

The eternal God is your refuge, and underneath
are the everlasting arms; He will thrust out the
enemy from before you, and will say, "Destroy!"
                              DEUTERONOMY 33:27

The baby carried in the arms of his mother
knows no fear, even though their path may lie
through a howling wilderness or through raging
enemies. The mother's arms are his impregnable
fortress. And the "everlasting arms" of God can be
no less.

In all their affliction He was afflicted, and the Angel of His Presence saved them; in His love and in
His pity He redeemed them; and He bore them
and carried them all the days of old.   ISAIAH 63:9

As an eagle stirs up its nest, hovers over its young,
spreading out its wings, taking them up, carrying

them on its wings, so the LORD alone led him, and there was no foreign god with him.

DEUTERONOMY 32:11–12

Even the eagle knows this secret of a mother's love. When the little eagles are old enough to learn to fly, she stirs up the nest and pushes them out, so that they are forced to use their wings. But she soars in the air under them and watches them with eyes of love. When she sees any little eaglet showing signs of fatigue, she flies beneath it and spreads out her great, strong mother wings to bear it up until it is rested and ready to fly again. "So the LORD" does with us.

Both men and animals instinctively recognize the mother's right and duty to bear the burden of the child she has brought into the world. Moses appealed to this universal instinct when he complained to the Lord concerning the children of Israel.

Did I conceive all these people? Did I beget them, that You should say to me, "Carry them in your bosom, as a guardian carries a nursing child," to the land which You swore to their fathers?

NUMBERS 11:12

In recounting the wilderness wandering, Moses used a similar illustration to describe how the Lord had dealt with the Israelites.

In the wilderness...you saw how the LORD your God carried you, as a man carries his son, in all the way that you went until you came to this place.

DEUTERONOMY 1:31

We cannot make any mistake, then, in believing that the Lord carries us in His arms and holds us close to His heart with far more tenderness and watchful care than any mother ever could.

HE DRIES OUR TEARS

The mother wipes away the tears of her little one.

For the Lamb who is in the midst of the throne will shepherd them and lead them to living fountains of waters. And God will wipe away every tear from their eyes.   REVELATION 7:17

Where do the little tearful darlings run for comfort except to their mothers? They know that no other hand can wipe away their tears as hers can. Have we not often seen children, when they were hurt, holding in their cries until Mother came, because they felt instinctively that nobody but Mother could sympathize or console?

Should we not, then, let our God wipe away the tears from our eyes and give us "joy for mourning" (Isaiah 61:3), just as we used to let our mothers do when we were in their loving care?

For You have delivered my soul from death, my eyes from tears, and my feet from falling.
                    PSALM 116:8

He will swallow up death forever, and the Lord GOD will wipe away tears from all faces; the rebuke of His people He will take away from all the earth; for the LORD has spoken.   ISAIAH 25:8

For the people shall dwell in Zion at Jerusalem;
you shall weep no more. He will be very gracious
to you at the sound of your cry; when He hears it,
He will answer you.   ISAIAH 30:19

Depart from me, all you workers of iniquity; for
the LORD has heard the voice of my weeping. The
LORD has heard my supplication; the LORD will receive my prayer.   PSALM 6:8–9

When our Lord was on earth, He was very tender toward the tears of His people.

When the Lord saw her, He had compassion on her
and said to her, "Do not weep."   LUKE 7:13

Now all wept and mourned for her; but He said,
"Do not weep; she is not dead, but sleeping."
                                         LUKE 8:52

Just as a mother says, "Darling, do not cry," so
God says to us, "Do not weep." Our tears give Him
grief.

Therefore, when Jesus saw her weeping, and the
Jews who came with her weeping, He groaned in
the spirit and was troubled.   JOHN 11:33

Perhaps we do not remember this fact enough,
and we sometimes indulge ourselves in weeping
when our Lord would gladly wipe away our tears.
Let us consider this truth and see if, for His sake as
for our mothers' sake, we cannot dry our eyes and
try to bear cheerfully the sorrows He permits to
come to us. Have we never known what it means to

restrain our sorrow so that we will not grieve a loved one? Should we not sometimes do this for our Lord?

But be glad and rejoice forever in what I create; for behold, I create Jerusalem as a rejoicing, and her people a joy. I will rejoice in Jerusalem, and joy in My people; the voice of weeping shall no longer be heard in her, nor the voice of crying.
ISAIAH 65:18–19

And God will wipe away every tear from their eyes; there shall be no more death, nor sorrow, nor crying. There shall be no more pain, for the former things have passed away.   REVELATION 21:4

HE TENDS TO US IN SICKNESS

The mother watches over her children in sickness and does all she can to comfort and to heal.

The LORD will strengthen him on his bed of illness; You will sustain him on his sickbed.
PSALM 41:3

When there is famine in the land, pestilence or blight or mildew, locusts or grasshoppers; when their enemy besieges them in the land of their cities; whatever plague or whatever sickness there is; whatever prayer, whatever supplication is made by anyone, or by all Your people Israel, when each one knows the plague of his own heart, and spreads out his hands toward this temple: then hear in heaven Your dwelling place, and forgive, and act, and give to everyone according to all his ways, whose heart You know (for You alone know the hearts of all the sons of men). 1 KINGS 8:37–39

Concerning our Lord, it was declared that He bore not only our sins, but also our sicknesses.

> When evening had come, they brought to Him many who were demon-possessed. And He cast out the spirits with a word, and healed all who were sick, that it might be fulfilled which was spoken by Isaiah the prophet, saying: "He Himself took our infirmities and bore our sicknesses."
>
> MATTHEW 8:16–17

The story of His life on earth is one continual record of His tenderness with sickness, and of His power and willingness to heal.

> And Jesus went about all Galilee, teaching in their synagogues, preaching the gospel of the kingdom, and healing all kinds of sickness and all kinds of disease among the people.   MATTHEW 4:23

> And when they came out of the boat, immediately the people recognized Him, ran through that whole surrounding region, and began to carry about on beds those who were sick to wherever they heard He was. Wherever He entered into villages, cities, or in the country, they laid the sick in the marketplaces, and begged Him that they might just touch the hem of His garment. And as many as touched Him were made well.   MARK 6:54–56

How literally we are to take this bearing of our sicknesses is a subject that we cannot consider here. There is a great difference of opinion on the matter. But of this I am sure: all who trust Him will find that the tenderest mother's love and care in sickness is only a faint picture of the love and care that He will bestow.

HE LOVES US IN SPITE OF OUR SIN

The mother bears with the naughty child as no one else can and loves him freely in spite of his sin.

Now it happened, as Jesus sat at the table in the house, that behold, many tax collectors and sinners came and sat down with Him and His disciples. And when the Pharisees saw it, they said to His disciples, "Why does your Teacher eat with tax collectors and sinners?" When Jesus heard that, He said to them, "Those who are well have no need of a physician, but those who are sick. But go and learn what this means: 'I desire mercy and not sacrifice.' For I did not come to call the righteous, but sinners, to repentance."   MATTHEW 9:10–13

Other people love us when we are good; our mothers love us when we are naughty. God is like our mothers.

But God demonstrates His own love toward us, in that while we were still sinners, Christ died for us.
ROMANS 5:8

This is a faithful saying and worthy of all acceptance, that Christ Jesus came into the world to save sinners, of whom I am chief.   1 TIMOTHY 1:15

Our mothers do not love our sins, but they love us, even when we are sinners. They love us enough to try to save us from our sins. This attitude is like God's.

> There's a wideness in God's mercy,
>   Like the wideness of the sea;
> There's a kindness in His justice
>   That is more than liberty.
>
> There's no place where earthly sorrows
>   Are more felt than up in heaven;
> There's no place where earthly failings
>   Have such kindly judgment given.

Only mothers can be just to their children, for they alone know their temptations. And only God can be just toward us, for He alone "knows our frame; He remembers that we are dust" (Psalm 103:14).

HE SACRIFICES LIFE ITSELF FOR US

A mother will lay down her life for her child, and our Lord laid down His life for us.

[Jesus said,] "I am the good shepherd. The good shepherd gives His life for the sheep. But a hireling, he who is not the shepherd, one who does not own the sheep, sees the wolf coming and leaves the sheep and flees; and the wolf catches the sheep and scatters them. The hireling flees because he is a hireling and does not care about the sheep. I am the good shepherd; and I know My sheep, and am known by My own. As the Father knows Me, even so I know the Father; and I lay down My life for the sheep." JOHN 10:11–15

By this we know love, because He laid down His life for us. And we also ought to lay down our lives for the brethren.   1 JOHN 3:16

> Love divine, of such great loving,
>   Only mothers know the cost;
> Cost of love, that, all love passing,
>   Gave itself to save the lost!

All nature teaches us this law of the self-sacrifice of motherhood. Even the wild mother tiger yields to its power. Concerning this animal, one writer said,

It is a tiger's impulse to resent an injury. Pluck her by the hair, strike her on the flank, she will leap upon and attack you. But to resent an injury is not her strongest impulse. Watch those helpless kitten creatures playing with her. They are so weak that a careless movement of her giant paw would destroy them, but she makes no careless movement. They have caused her a hundredfold the pain your blow would produce, yet she does not repay evil for evil. These puny mites of helpless impotence she strokes, with love's light in her eyes; she licks the shapeless forms of her tormentors, and, as they plunge at her, each groan of her anguish is transformed by love into a whinny of delight. She moves her massive head in a way that shows that He who bade you turn the other cheek created her. When strong enough to rise, the terrible creature goes forth to sacrifice herself for her own. She will starve so that they may thrive. She is formidable for her little ones, as Christ is formidable for His. He who made her, taught her the secret of motherhood.

The little Bantam hen knows the same secret. She will spread her tiny wings and rush to her death if her little chicks are in danger.

In all of creation, the beautiful law of motherhood points to the grandeur of an utter self-sacrifice. Moreover, He who created motherhood cannot Himself do less than the mothers He has made.

For when we were still without strength, in due time Christ died for the ungodly.   ROMANS 5:6

For God did not appoint us to wrath, but to obtain salvation through our Lord Jesus Christ, who died for us, that whether we wake or sleep, we should live together with Him.   1 THESSALONIANS 5:9–10

For the love of Christ compels us, because we judge thus: that if One died for all, then all died; and He died for all, that those who live should live no longer for themselves, but for Him who died for them and rose again.   2 CORINTHIANS 5:14–15

Someone once made the following observation about nature:

When the polar bear lays down her life for the cub that cannot live without her; when the leopard gives herself to death in defense of her helpless whelp, the Arctic Circle and the Libyan Desert unite in declaring that the spirit of nature is the spirit of Christ.

HE DIRECTS US IN THE RIGHT ROAD

The mother holds the hand of her child to lead him in the right path. She lifts him over the rough places so that he will not stumble.

For He shall give His angels charge over you, to keep you in all your ways. In their hands they shall bear you up, lest you dash your foot against a stone.   PSALM 91:11–12

He will guard the feet of His saints.   1 SAMUEL 2:9

Now to Him who is able to keep you from stumbling, and to present you faultless before the presence of His glory with exceeding joy.   JUDE 24

For the LORD will be your confidence, and will keep your foot from being caught.   PROVERBS 3:26

It is the mother who holds the child, not the other way around. It is the mother who watches the path and lifts the baby's feet over the stones and obstacles that obstruct the way. The responsibility is all hers. The child only has to abandon himself to her leading and trust her fully. In the same way, our God "knows the way that [we] take" (Job 23:10) and will "direct all [our] ways" (Isaiah 45:13) if we will only commit ourselves to His care.

He will not allow your foot to be moved; He who keeps you will not slumber.   PSALM 121:3

My eyes are ever toward the LORD, for He shall pluck my feet out of the net.   PSALM 25:15

He also brought me up out of a horrible pit, out of the miry clay, and set my feet upon a rock, and established my steps.   PSALM 40:2

You have also given me the shield of Your salvation; Your right hand has held me up, Your gentleness has made me great. You enlarged my path under me, so my feet did not slip.   PSALM 18:35–36

Uphold my steps in Your paths, that my footsteps may not slip.   PSALM 17:5

No matter how much the child may resist the mother's leading or wander from her loving grasp, still she is always ready to again take hold of his hand and lead him.

If I take the wings of the morning, and dwell in the uttermost parts of the sea, even there Your hand shall lead me, and Your right hand shall hold me.   PSALM 139:9–10

For I, the LORD your God, will hold your right hand, saying to you, "Fear not, I will help you."
ISAIAH 41:13

HE FEEDS US WHEN WE HUNGER

The mother is always ready to feed her hungry child. She herself would starve before she would allow the child to go hungry.

The eyes of all look expectantly to You, and You give them their food in due season. You open Your hand and satisfy the desire of every living thing.
PSALM 145:15–16

Blessed are those who hunger and thirst for righteousness, for they shall be filled.   MATTHEW 5:6

For He satisfies the longing soul, and fills the
hungry soul with goodness.   PSALM 107:9

The wise mother does not always give the child
the food that he asks for. Sometimes such food would
be disastrous to his health. But she always gives the
food that is best for him, to the extent of her knowledge and ability. And we may be perfectly sure that
our God always gives us what is best, whether it is
what we ask for or not. Therefore, we must be satisfied.

My soul shall be satisfied as with marrow and fat-
ness, and my mouth shall praise You with joyful
lips.   PSALM 63:5

[Jesus said,] "If a son asks for bread from any father among you, will he give him a stone? Or if he
asks for a fish, will he give him a serpent instead
of a fish? Or if he asks for an egg, will he offer him
a scorpion? If you then, being evil, know how to
give good gifts to your children, how much more
will your heavenly Father give the Holy Spirit to
those who ask Him!"   LUKE 11:11–13

What our Father gives us may look to us like a
"serpent" or a "scorpion," but since He gives it, we
may be sure it cannot be anything but the best thing
for us. If parents know how to give good gifts, how
much more must He?

[Jesus said,] "Therefore I say to you, do not worry
about your life, what you will eat or what you will
drink; nor about your body, what you will put on.

173

Is not life more than food and the body more than clothing? Look at the birds of the air, for they neither sow nor reap nor gather into barns; yet your heavenly Father feeds them. Are you not of more value than they?...Therefore do not worry, saying, 'What shall we eat?' or 'What shall we drink?' or 'What shall we wear?' For after all these things the Gentiles seek. For your heavenly Father knows that you need all these things. But seek first the kingdom of God and His righteousness, and all these things shall be added to you."

MATTHEW 6:25–26, 31–33

The child does not have to supply or prepare his own food; this is the mother's responsibility. All the child has to do is eat and live, without care and without cost.

Ho! Everyone who thirsts, come to the waters; and you who have no money, come, buy and eat. Yes, come, buy wine and milk without money and without price. Why do you spend money for what is not bread, and your wages for what does not satisfy? Listen carefully to Me, and eat what is good, and let your soul delight itself in abundance.

ISAIAH 55:1–2

HE KEEPS US CLEAN AND WELL-DRESSED

The mother takes pleasure in her child and loves to keep him clean and dress him attractively.

For the LORD takes pleasure in His people; He will beautify the humble with salvation.   PSALM 149:4

174

I will greatly rejoice in the LORD, my soul shall be joyful in my God; for He has clothed me with the garments of salvation, He has covered me with the robe of righteousness, as a bridegroom decks himself with ornaments, and as a bride adorns herself with her jewels.   ISAIAH 61:10

What joy in all the world is equal to the joy of a mother in her child? What job is sweeter to her than to dress him up in nice clothes?

Yet it is hard for the children themselves to believe this. They do not know the mother's heart, and they cannot enter into her joy in them.

It is the same with us toward our God. We cannot believe that He can take pleasure in such poor miserable creatures as we are. We know that we delight in Him, but it seems impossible for Him to delight in us.

Yet, in spite of all the child's ignorance of it, the mother *does* take joy in her little ones; and in spite of our doubts and fears, God *does* rejoice in us.

The LORD takes pleasure in those who fear Him, in those who hope in His mercy.   PSALM 147:11

Therefore, cannot we, who understand something of the mother's heart toward her children, understand something of the heart of God toward us?

"Yes, I swore an oath to you and entered into a covenant with you, and you became Mine," says the Lord GOD. "Then I washed you in water; yes, I thoroughly washed off your blood, and I anointed you with oil. I clothed you in embroidered cloth

175

and gave you sandals of badger skin; I clothed you with fine linen and covered you with silk. I adorned you with ornaments, put bracelets on your wrists, and a chain on your neck. And I put a jewel in your nose, earrings in your ears, and a beautiful crown on your head. Thus you were adorned with gold and silver, and your clothing was of fine linen, silk, and embroidered cloth. You ate pastry of fine flour, honey, and oil. You were exceedingly beautiful, and succeeded to royalty. Your fame went out among the nations because of your beauty, for it was perfect through My splendor which I had bestowed on you," says the Lord GOD.   EZEKIEL 16:8–14

The royal daughter is all glorious within the palace; her clothing is woven with gold. She shall be brought to the King in robes of many colors; the virgins, her companions who follow her, shall be brought to You.   PSALM 45:13–14

The child does not make his own clothes, but leaves that responsibility to the mother.

[Jesus said,] "So why do you worry about clothing? Consider the lilies of the field, how they grow: they neither toil nor spin; and yet I say to you that even Solomon in all his glory was not arrayed like one of these. Now if God so clothes the grass of the field, which today is, and tomorrow is thrown into the oven, will He not much more clothe you, O you of little faith?"   MATTHEW 6:28–30

It would grieve the mother to see her little one anxious and troubled about his clothing, and it grieves our God to see us that way. Moreover, all our efforts to clothe ourselves are utter failures, just as the child's would be.

And when you are plundered, what will you do? Though you clothe yourself with crimson, though you adorn yourself with ornaments of gold, though you enlarge your eyes with paint, in vain you will make yourself fair; your lovers will despise you; they will seek your life. JEREMIAH 4:30

Only the Lord can clothe us, and only He can make us clean.

"Come now, and let us reason together," says the LORD, "though your sins are like scarlet, they shall be as white as snow; though they are red like crimson, they shall be as wool." ISAIAH 1:18

But if we walk in the light as He is in the light, we have fellowship with one another, and the blood of Jesus Christ His Son cleanses us from all sin. 1 JOHN 1:7

If we confess our sins, He is faithful and just to forgive us our sins and to cleanse us from all un-righteousness. 1 JOHN 1:9

HE SHOWS TENDER SYMPATHY

The mother feels the hurts and sufferings of her child as though they were her own.

In all their affliction He was afflicted, and the An-gel of His Presence saved them; in His love and in

His pity He redeemed them; and He bore them and carried them all the days of old.   ISAIAH 63:9

Even though the affliction may be the result of sin, still the mother grieves over it and longs to remedy it. Strangers may say, "It serves you right," but no good mother ever could.

For we do not have a High Priest who cannot sympathize with our weaknesses, but was in all points tempted as we are, yet without sin.
                                            HEBREWS 4:15

He who touches you touches the apple of His eye.
                                            ZECHARIAH 2:8

HE NEVER DESERTS US

The mother cannot forget or forsake her child. Yet even this may be possible with a human mother, but with God never!

But Zion said, "The LORD has forsaken me, and my Lord has forgotten me." "Can a woman forget her nursing child, and not have compassion on the son of her womb? Surely they may forget, yet I will not forget you. See, I have inscribed you on the palms of My hands; your walls are continually before Me."   ISAIAH 49:14–16

Why do you say, O Jacob, and speak, O Israel: "My way is hidden from the LORD, and my just claim is passed over by my God"? Have you not known? Have you not heard? The everlasting God, the

LORD, the Creator of the ends of the earth, neither
faints nor is weary. His understanding is un-
searchable. He gives power to the weak, and to
those who have no might He increases strength.
                                    ISAIAH 40:27–29

Christians sometimes talk as though God had
forsaken them, but this is impossible, for He has
said, "I will never leave you nor forsake you."

Let your conduct be without covetousness; be content with such things as you have. For He Himself
has said, "I will never leave you nor forsake you."
So we may boldly say: "The LORD is my helper; I
will not fear. What can man do to me?"
                                    HEBREWS 13:5–6

Be strong and of good courage, do not fear nor be
afraid of them; for the LORD your God, He is the
One who goes with you. He will not leave you nor
forsake you....And the LORD, He is the one who
goes before you. He will be with you, He will not
leave you nor forsake you; do not fear nor be dismayed.   DEUTERONOMY 31:6, 8

The child who is delirious thinks his mother
has forsaken him, although all the time she is close
beside him. And we, in the delirium of our doubts
and fears, think just as falsely that God has forsaken us.

For the LORD will not forsake His people, for His
great name's sake, because it has pleased the
LORD to make you His people.   1 SAMUEL 12:22

And I will dwell among the children of Israel, and will not forsake My people Israel.   1 KINGS 6:13

No man shall be able to stand before you all the days of your life; as I was with Moses, so I will be with you. I will not leave you nor forsake you.
JOSHUA 1:5

The poor and needy seek water, but there is none, their tongues fail for thirst. I, the LORD, will hear them; I, the God of Israel, will not forsake them.
ISAIAH 41:17

HE DEFENDS US IN DANGER

The mother stays beside her child when he is in danger, even though all others may abandon him.

[Jesus said,] "I am the good shepherd. The good shepherd gives His life for the sheep. But a hireling, he who is not the shepherd, one who does not own the sheep, sees the wolf coming and leaves the sheep and flees; and the wolf catches the sheep and scatters them. The hireling flees because he is a hireling and does not care about the sheep."
JOHN 10:11–13

A hired nurse, though she may be paid ever so much salary, may flee in a moment of danger and leave the baby to his fate. But danger only makes the mother stay closer to her helpless little one. The mother hen, who generally flees at the first approach of danger, will stand as firm and dauntless as a lion if she has her little chicks to guard.

Have we ever dared to think of our Lord as though He were a "hireling" who flees when danger approaches? Have we not even been more ready to trust earthly "hirelings" than to trust Him at times?

The LORD also will be a refuge for the oppressed, a refuge in times of trouble.   PSALM 9:9

For in the time of trouble He shall hide me in His pavilion; in the secret place of His tabernacle He shall hide me; He shall set me high upon a rock.
                                                   PSALM 27:5

HE LOOKS FOR THE LOST

If the child is lost, the mother leaves everything to look for him and never gives up until she finds him.

So He spoke this parable to them, saying: "What man of you, having a hundred sheep, if he loses one of them, does not leave the ninety-nine in the wilderness, and go after the one which is lost until he finds it? And when he has found it, he lays it on his shoulders, rejoicing. And when he comes home, he calls together his friends and neighbors, saying to them, 'Rejoice with me, for I have found my sheep which was lost!' I say to you that likewise there will be more joy in heaven over one sinner who repents than over ninety-nine just persons who need no repentance. Or what woman, having ten silver coins, if she loses one coin, does not light a lamp, sweep the house, and search carefully until she finds it? And when she has found it, she calls her friends and neighbors together, saying, 'Rejoice with me, for I have found the piece which I lost!' Likewise, I say to you, there is joy in the presence of the angels of God over one sinner who repents."   LUKE 15:3–10

[Jesus said,] "For the Son of Man has come to save that which was lost. What do you think? If a man has a hundred sheep, and one of them goes astray, does he not leave the ninety-nine and go to the mountains to seek the one that is straying? And if he should find it, assuredly, I say to you, he rejoices more over that sheep than over the ninety-nine that did not go astray. Even so it is not the will of your Father who is in heaven that one of these little ones should perish."
                                        MATTHEW 18:11–14

For thus says the Lord GOD: "Indeed I Myself will search for My sheep and seek them out. As a shepherd seeks out his flock on the day he is among his scattered sheep, so will I seek out My sheep and deliver them from all the places where they were scattered on a cloudy and dark day."
                                        EZEKIEL 34:11–12

What, then, is the summary of the whole matter? Simply this: Even if God were only as good as the mothers He has made, where could there be any room for worry or fear? Furthermore, since He is much truer to the ideal of motherhood than an earthly mother can be—to the degree that His infiniteness is far above hers—what oceans and continents of bliss are ours for the taking! Will we not take them?

Chapter 10

As a Little Child

Then they also brought infants to Him that He might touch them; but when the disciples saw it, they rebuked them. But Jesus called them to Him and said, "Let the little children come to Me, and do not forbid them; for of such is the kingdom of God. Assuredly, I say to you, whoever does not receive the kingdom of God as a little child will by no means enter it."
—Luke 18:15–17

Notice that, in verse fifteen, the word used to describe the little children whom our Lord here gave as an example is "infants." In verse sixteen, He said concerning them, "Of such is the kingdom of God."

In that hour Jesus rejoiced in the Spirit and said, "I thank You, Father, Lord of heaven and earth, that You have hidden these things from the wise and prudent and revealed them to babes. Even so, Father, for so it seemed good in Your sight."

LUKE 10:21

183

At that time the disciples came to Jesus, saying, "Who then is greatest in the kingdom of heaven?" Then Jesus called a little child to Him, set him in the midst of them, and said, "Assuredly, I say to you, unless you are converted and become as little children, you will by no means enter the kingdom of heaven. Therefore whoever humbles himself as this little child is the greatest in the kingdom of heaven."   MATTHEW 18:1–4

Little children, "infants," are to be our example. Neither grown-up children nor half-grown ones—not precocious children, children who have old heads on young shoulders—but real, honest, downright little children. These small ones have all the characteristics of "childness"—the candid, impulsive, tender, trustful, self-forgetting, carefree spirit of a little child.

CHARACTERISTICS OF A CHILD

It is vital, then, that we get a true idea of what it means to be a little child. We must know the characteristics of ideal childhood, for these are the qualities that we must have if we are to become "as little children."

No Worries

A little child has no anxiety about the supply of his needs, but he leaves all the concerns of providing to his parents. Likewise, we must not worry about the supply of our needs but must leave the whole burden of providing to our heavenly Father.

[Jesus said,] "Therefore I say to you, do not worry about your life, what you will eat or what you will drink; nor about your body, what you will put on. Is not life more than food and the body more than clothing? Look at the birds of the air, for they neither sow nor reap nor gather into barns; yet your heavenly Father feeds them. Are you not of more value than they?"   MATTHEW 6:25–26

[Jesus said,] "Therefore do not worry, saying, 'What shall we eat?' or 'What shall we drink?' or 'What shall we wear?' For after all these things the Gentiles seek. For your heavenly Father knows that you need all these things. But seek first the kingdom of God and His righteousness, and all these things shall be added to you."
                                    MATTHEW 6:31–33

Casting all your care upon Him, for He cares for you.   1 PETER 5:7

No Concern about Tomorrow

A little child lives in the present moment and leaves the planning of his future to the parent. We also must live in the present moment and leave our future to God.

[Jesus said,] "Therefore do not worry about tomorrow, for tomorrow will worry about its own things. Sufficient for the day is its own trouble."
                                    MATTHEW 6:34

Unafraid to Ask

A little child asks for everything he wants without formality, and in joyous confidence of being heard and answered. We must ask in unceremonious, childlike confidence for everything we want, sure of being heard and answered, according to God's divine wisdom.

> Be anxious for nothing, but in everything by prayer and supplication, with thanksgiving, let your requests be made known to God.
> PHILIPPIANS 4:6

> [Jesus said,] "If you abide in Me, and My words abide in you, you will ask what you desire, and it shall be done for you." JOHN 15:7

> [Jesus said,] "Therefore I say to you, whatever things you ask when you pray, believe that you receive them, and you will have them." MARK 11:24

> [Jesus said,] "Ask, and it will be given to you; seek, and you will find; knock, and it will be opened to you. For everyone who asks receives, and he who seeks finds, and to him who knocks it will be opened. Or what man is there among you who, if his son asks for bread, will give him a stone? Or if he asks for a fish, will he give him a serpent? If you then, being evil, know how to give good gifts to your children, how much more will your Father who is in heaven give good things to those who ask Him!" MATTHEW 7:7–11

Readily Comforted

The little child runs to his mother for comfort in all his troubles. In the same way, we must go to our Lord for comfort in all our troubles.

For thus says the LORD: "Behold, I will extend peace to her [Jerusalem] like a river, and the glory of the Gentiles like a flowing stream. Then you shall feed; on her sides shall you be carried, and be dandled on her knees. As one whom his mother comforts, so I will comfort you; and you shall be comforted in Jerusalem." ISAIAH 66:12–13

Blessed be the God and Father of our Lord Jesus Christ, the Father of mercies and God of all comfort, who comforts us in all our tribulation, that we may be able to comfort those who are in any trouble, with the comfort with which we ourselves are comforted by God. 2 CORINTHIANS 1:3–4

Safe from All Foes

The little child looks to his father and mother to rescue him from anyone who would seek to harm him. Likewise, we must look to our God for deliverance from our enemies.

For He will deliver the needy when he cries, the poor also, and him who has no helper. PSALM 72:12

Then they cried out to the LORD in their trouble, and He delivered them out of their distresses. PSALM 107:6

This poor man cried out, and the LORD heard him, and saved him out of all his troubles. PSALM 34:6

Our fathers trusted in You; they trusted, and You delivered them. They cried to You, and were delivered; they trusted in You, and were not ashamed. PSALM 22:4–5

Willing to Relax

A little child rests in his mother's arms when he is weary. In the same way, we must rest our weary souls in the arms of God.

[Jesus said,] "Come to Me, all you who labor and are heavy laden, and I will give you rest."
MATTHEW 11:28

My people will dwell in a peaceful habitation, in secure dwellings, and in quiet resting places.
ISAIAH 32:18

For thus says the Lord GOD, the Holy One of Israel: "In returning and rest you shall be saved; in quietness and confidence shall be your strength."
ISAIAH 30:15

Curious and Confident

The little child asks questions about everything he wants to know. He believes all that his mother says, without question or doubt.

Likewise, we must ask our Lord about everything for which we need wisdom. We must believe all that He says with implicit confidence.

If any of you lacks wisdom, let him ask of God, who gives to all liberally and without reproach, and it will be given to him. But let him ask in faith, with no doubting, for he who doubts is like a wave of the sea driven and tossed by the wind. For let not that man suppose that he will receive anything from the Lord.
JAMES 1:5–7

Yes, if you cry out for discernment, and lift up your voice for understanding, if you seek her as silver, and search for her as for hidden treasures; then you will understand the fear of the LORD, and find the knowledge of God. For the LORD gives wisdom; from His mouth come knowledge and understanding.   PROVERBS 2:3–6

[Jesus said,] "But the Helper, the Holy Spirit, whom the Father will send in My name, He will teach you all things, and bring to your remembrance all things that I said to you."   JOHN 14:26

Certain of Triumph

The little child expects his father and mother to fight all his battles. He is always confident that they can conquer.

In the same way, we must expect our Lord to fight all our battles. We must be confident of His certain victory.

And Moses said to the people, "Do not be afraid. Stand still, and see the salvation of the LORD, which He will accomplish for you today. For the Egyptians whom you see today, you shall see again no more forever. The LORD will fight for you, and you shall hold your peace."   EXODUS 14:13–14

When you go out to battle against your enemies, and see horses and chariots and people more numerous than you, do not be afraid of them; for the LORD your God is with you, who brought you up from the land of Egypt. So it shall be, when you are on the verge of battle, that the priest shall approach and speak to the people. And he shall say to them, "Hear, O Israel: Today you are on the verge of battle with your enemies. Do not let your heart faint, do not be afraid, and do not tremble or be terrified because of them; for the LORD your God is He who goes with you, to fight for you against your enemies, to save you." DEUTERONOMY 20:1–4

Beloved, do not avenge yourselves, but rather give place to wrath; for it is written, "Vengeance is Mine, I will repay," says the Lord. ROMANS 12:19

Through God we will do valiantly, for it is He who shall tread down our enemies. PSALM 60:12

Then Moses and the children of Israel sang this song to the LORD, and spoke, saying: "I will sing to the LORD, for He has triumphed gloriously! The horse and its rider He has thrown into the sea! The LORD is my strength and song, and He has become my salvation; He is my God, and I will praise Him; my father's God, and I will exalt Him. The LORD is a man of war; the LORD is His name."
EXODUS 15:1–3

Seeks a Sure Sanctuary

The little child takes refuge in his mother's arms when an enemy approaches. He is afraid of nothing in her presence. Likewise, we must make the Lord our refuge and must fear nothing in His presence.

The eternal God is your refuge, and underneath are the everlasting arms; He will thrust out the enemy from before you, and will say, "Destroy!"
DEUTERONOMY 33:27

The LORD is my light and my salvation; whom shall I fear? The LORD is the strength of my life; of whom shall I be afraid? When the wicked came against me to eat up my flesh, my enemies and foes, they stumbled and fell. Though an army may encamp against me, my heart shall not fear; though war should rise against me, in this I will be confident. PSALM 27:1-3

God is our refuge and strength, a very present help in trouble. Therefore we will not fear, even though the earth be removed, and though the mountains be carried into the midst of the sea; though its waters roar and be troubled, though the mountains shake with its swelling. PSALM 46:1-3

I will say of the LORD, "He is my refuge and my fortress; my God, in Him I will trust." Surely He shall deliver you from the snare of the fowler and from the perilous pestilence. He shall cover you with His feathers, and under His wings you shall take refuge; His truth shall be your shield and buckler. You shall not be afraid of the terror by night, nor of the arrow that flies by day, nor of the pestilence that walks in darkness, nor of the destruction that lays waste at noonday. A thousand may fall at your side, and ten thousand at your right hand; but it shall not come near you. Only with your eyes shall you look, and see the reward of the wicked. Because you have made the LORD, who is my refuge, even the Most High, your dwelling place, no evil shall befall you, nor shall any plague come near your dwelling. PSALM 91:2-10

The LORD also will be a refuge for the oppressed, a refuge in times of trouble. And those who know Your name will put their trust in You; for You, LORD, have not forsaken those who seek You.

PSALM 9:9–10

Unbridled Assurance

The little child believes his parents can do everything and that nothing is too hard for them. In the same way, we must believe that all things are possible for our Father in heaven, and that nothing can thwart His blessed will.

He [Abraham] did not waver at the promise of God through unbelief, but was strengthened in faith, giving glory to God, and being fully convinced that what He had promised He was also able to perform. ROMANS 4:20–21

Then the disciples came to Jesus privately and said, "Why could we not cast it [the demon] out?" So Jesus said to them, "Because of your unbelief; for assuredly, I say to you, if you have faith as a mustard seed, you will say to this mountain, 'Move from here to there,' and it will move; and nothing will be impossible for you." MATTHEW 17:19–20

Jesus said to him, "If you can believe, all things are possible to him who believes." MARK 9:23

And when He had come into the house, the blind men came to Him. And Jesus said to them, "Do you believe that I am able to do this?" They said to

Him, "Yes, Lord." Then He touched their eyes,
saying, "According to your faith let it be to you."
MATTHEW 9:28–29

Ready to Receive

The little child is never surprised at the great-
ness of any gift that his parents may offer. He never
hesitates, because of foolish mistrust, to accept the
most lavish presents.

Similarly, we must not be hindered by a foolish
mistrust in accepting eagerly and gladly the lavish
gifts that our Lord is continually seeking to bestow
upon us.

I am the LORD your God, who brought you out of
the land of Egypt; open your mouth wide, and I
will fill it. PSALM 81:10

For if by the one man's [Adam's] offense death
reigned through the one, much more those who receive abundance of grace and of the gift of righteousness will reign in life through the One, Jesus
Christ. ROMANS 5:17

But as it is written: "Eye has not seen, nor ear
heard, nor have entered into the heart of man the
things which God has prepared for those who love
Him." But God has revealed them to us through
His Spirit. For the Spirit searches all things, yes,
the deep things of God. 1 CORINTHIANS 2:9–10

Now to Him who is able to do exceedingly abundantly above all that we ask or think, according to

the power that works in us, to Him be glory in the
church by Christ Jesus to all generations, forever
and ever. Amen.   EPHESIANS 3:20–21

Always Trusting

The little child never doubts the love and care of
his mother. He would be extremely surprised if there
were any lack.

We also must never doubt the love and care of
our Lord, or be surprised at His tender watchfulness
over all our needs.

[Jesus said,] "Now if God so clothes the grass of
the field, which today is, and tomorrow is thrown
into the oven, will He not much more clothe you, O
you of little faith?"   MATTHEW 6:30

Jesus…said to them, "O you of little faith, why do
you reason among yourselves because you have
brought no bread? Do you not yet understand, or
remember the five loaves of the five thousand and
how many baskets you took up? Nor the seven
loaves of the four thousand and how many large
baskets you took up?"   MATTHEW 16:8–10

On the same day, when evening had come, He said
to them, "Let us cross over to the other side." Now
when they had left the multitude, they took Him
along in the boat as He was. And other little boats
were also with Him. And a great windstorm arose,
and the waves beat into the boat, so that it was already filling. But He was in the stern, asleep on a
pillow. And they awoke Him and said to Him,
"Teacher, do You not care that we are perishing?"

Then He arose and rebuked the wind, and said to the sea, "Peace, be still!" And the wind ceased and there was a great calm. But He said to them, "Why are you so fearful? How is it that you have no faith?"   MARK 4:35–40

[Jesus said,] "Let not your heart be troubled; you believe in God, believe also in Me. In My Father's house are many mansions; if it were not so, I would have told you. I go to prepare a place for you. And if I go and prepare a place for you, I will come again and receive you to Myself; that where I am, there you may be also."   JOHN 14:1–3

Yes, they spoke against God: they said, "Can God prepare a table in the wilderness? Behold, He struck the rock, so that the waters gushed out, and the streams overflowed. Can He give bread also? Can He provide meat for His people?" Therefore the LORD heard this and was furious; so a fire was kindled against Jacob, and anger also came up against Israel, because they did not believe in God, and did not trust in His salvation. Yet He had commanded the clouds above, and opened the doors of heaven, had rained down manna on them to eat, and given them of the bread of heaven.
PSALM 78:19–24

No Questions or Complaints

The little child is content with the arrangements his mother makes for him and asks no questions.

We, likewise, must be content with our Lord's arrangements for us. We must not ask any questions or murmur about the situations He may permit.

Let your conduct be without covetousness; be content with such things as you have. For He Himself has said, "I will never leave you nor forsake you."

HEBREWS 13:5

But indeed, O man, who are you to reply against God? Will the thing formed say to him who formed it, "Why have you made me like this?"

ROMANS 9:20

Then all the congregation of the children of Israel set out on their journey from the Wilderness of Sin, according to the commandment of the LORD, and camped in Rephidim; but there was no water for the people to drink. Therefore the people contended with Moses, and said, "Give us water, that we may drink." And Moses said to them, "Why do you contend with me? Why do you tempt the LORD?" And the people thirsted there for water, and the people complained against Moses, and said, "Why is it you have brought us up out of Egypt, to kill us and our children and our livestock with thirst?"...So he called the name of the place Massah [Tempted] and Meribah [Contention], because of the contention of the children of Israel, and because they tempted the LORD, saying, "Is the LORD among us or not?"   EXODUS 17:1–3, 7

[Do not] complain, as some of them [the Israelites] also complained, and were destroyed by the destroyer. Now all these things happened to them as examples, and they were written for our admonition, upon whom the ends of the ages have come.

1 CORINTHIANS 10:10–11

Not that I speak in regard to need, for I have learned in whatever state I am, to be content: I know how to be abased, and I know how to abound. Everywhere and in all things I have learned both to be full and to be hungry, both to abound and to suffer need.   PHILIPPIANS 4:11–12

Now godliness with contentment is great gain. For we brought nothing into this world, and it is certain we can carry nothing out. And having food and clothing, with these we shall be content.
1 TIMOTHY 6:6–8

Flourishing Freely

Little children grow as the flowers grow, without any thought about their development. In the same way, we must "consider the lilies...how they grow" and grow like them, without anxiety or strain.

[Jesus said,] "Which of you by worrying can add one cubit to his stature? So why do you worry about clothing? Consider the lilies of the field, how they grow: they neither toil nor spin; and yet I say to you that even Solomon in all his glory was not arrayed like one of these."   MATTHEW 6:27–29

As newborn babes, desire the pure milk of the word, that you may grow thereby.   1 PETER 2:2

I will be like the dew to Israel; he shall grow like the lily, and lengthen his roots like Lebanon. His branches shall spread; his beauty shall be like an olive tree, and his fragrance like Lebanon.
HOSEA 14:5–6

The righteous shall flourish like a palm tree, he shall grow like a cedar in Lebanon. Those who are planted in the house of the LORD shall flourish in the courts of our God. They shall still bear fruit in old age; they shall be fresh and flourishing.
PSALM 92:12–14

Blessed is the man who trusts in the LORD, and whose hope is the LORD. For he shall be like a tree planted by the waters, which spreads out its roots by the river, and will not fear when heat comes; but its leaf will be green, and will not be anxious in the year of drought, nor will cease from yielding fruit.
JEREMIAH 17:7–8

Sure of a Warm Reception

The little child comes confidently into his mother's presence and never doubts her loving welcome. Likewise, we must come boldly into the presence of our Lord, without a question or doubt of His loving welcome.

For we do not have a High Priest who cannot sympathize with our weaknesses, but was in all points tempted as we are, yet without sin. Let us therefore come boldly to the throne of grace, that we may obtain mercy and find grace to help in time of need.
HEBREWS 4:15–16

Therefore, brethren, having boldness to enter the Holiest by the blood of Jesus, by a new and living way which He consecrated for us, through the veil, that is, His flesh, and having a High Priest over the house of God, let us draw near with a true heart in full assurance of faith, having our hearts sprinkled from an evil conscience and our bodies washed with pure water. Let us hold fast the confession of our hope without wavering, for He who promised is faithful.   HEBREWS 10:19–23

In [Christ Jesus our Lord] we have boldness and access with confidence through faith in Him.
                                        EPHESIANS 3:12

And we have known and believed the love that God has for us. God is love, and he who abides in love abides in God, and God in him. Love has been perfected among us in this: that we may have boldness in the day of judgment; because as He is, so are we in this world. There is no fear in love; but perfect love casts out fear, because fear involves torment. But he who fears has not been made perfect in love.   1 JOHN 4:16–18

So we may boldly say: "The LORD is my helper; I will not fear. What can man do to me?"
                                        HEBREWS 13:6

Constantly Praising

The little child boasts about his parents and wants to tell everyone of their goodness. In the same way, we must "make [our] boast in the LORD" and speak of His wonderful goodness whenever we can.

I will bless the LORD at all times; His praise shall continually be in my mouth. My soul shall make its boast in the LORD; the humble shall hear of it and be glad. Oh, magnify the LORD with me, and let us exalt His name together.   PSALM 34:1–3

Rejoice in the LORD, O you righteous! For praise from the upright is beautiful. Praise the LORD with the harp; make melody to Him with an instrument of ten strings. Sing to Him a new song; play skillfully with a shout of joy.   PSALM 33:1–3

In God we boast all day long, and praise Your name forever.   PSALM 44:8

Jesus...said to him [a demoniac whom he had delivered], "Go home to your friends, and tell them what great things the Lord has done for you, and how He has had compassion on you." And he departed and began to proclaim in Decapolis all that Jesus had done for him; and all marveled.
                                            MARK 5:19–20

I will mention the lovingkindnesses of the LORD and the praises of the LORD, according to all that the LORD has bestowed on us, and the great goodness toward the house of Israel, which He has bestowed on them according to His mercies, according to the multitude of His lovingkindnesses.
                                            ISAIAH 63:7

Open to Correction

Little children are punished when they are naughty. The punishment subdues and softens them, and they kiss the hand that disciplines them.

Similarly, the Lord chastises us when we misbehave, and we must accept His correction with thankful submission, letting it work in our spirits the intended blessing.

[Jesus said,] "As many as I love, I rebuke and chasten. Therefore be zealous and repent."

REVELATION 3:19

Behold, happy is the man whom God corrects; therefore do not despise the chastening of the Almighty. For He bruises, but He binds up; He wounds, but His hands make whole. JOB 5:17–18

And you have forgotten the exhortation which speaks to you as to sons: "My son, do not despise the chastening of the LORD, nor be discouraged when you are rebuked by Him; for whom the LORD loves He chastens, and scourges every son whom He receives." If you endure chastening, God deals with you as with sons; for what son is there whom a father does not chasten? But if you are without chastening, of which all have become partakers, then you are illegitimate and not sons. Furthermore, we have had human fathers who corrected us, and we paid them respect. Shall we not much more readily be in subjection to the Father of spirits and live? For they indeed for a few days chastened us as seemed best to them, but He for our profit, that we may be partakers of His holiness. Now no chastening seems to be joyful for the present, but painful; nevertheless, afterward it yields the peaceable fruit of righteousness to those who have been trained by it. HEBREWS 12:5–11

Enthusiastic about Instruction

Little children are teachable and eager to learn. We also must have teachable spirits and be eager to be taught by God.

A wise son heeds his father's instruction, but a scoffer does not listen to rebuke.   PROVERBS 13:1

How sweet are Your words to my taste, sweeter than honey to my mouth! Through Your precepts I get understanding; therefore I hate every false way.   PSALM 119:103–104

Whoever loves instruction loves knowledge, but he who hates correction is stupid.   PROVERBS 12:1

Oh, how I love Your law! It is my meditation all the day. You, through Your commandments, make me wiser than my enemies; for they are ever with me. I have more understanding than all my teachers, for Your testimonies are my meditation. I understand more than the ancients, because I keep Your precepts. I have restrained my feet from every evil way, that I may keep Your word. I have not departed from Your judgments, for You Yourself have taught me.   PSALM 119:97–102

[Jesus said,] "But the Helper, the Holy Spirit, whom the Father will send in My name, He will teach you all things, and bring to your remembrance all things that I said to you."   JOHN 14:26

[Jesus said,] "I still have many things to say to you, but you cannot bear them now. However, when He, the Spirit of truth, has come, He will guide you into all truth; for He will not speak on His own authority, but whatever He hears He will speak; and He will tell you things to come."
JOHN 16:12–13

Eager to Be of Assistance

The little child readily assists his mother in her work. We also must have ready feet to carry out our Father's business.

I will run the course of Your commandments, for You shall enlarge my heart. PSALM 119:32

I thought about my ways, and turned my feet to Your testimonies. I made haste, and did not delay to keep Your commandments. PSALM 119:59–60

Submissive to the One in Charge

Little children have obedient spirits and do what their parents desire, not what they themselves may think best.

We, likewise, must have obedient spirits to do God's will, not our own—no matter how much better our own plans may seem to us.

Then Samuel said [to King Saul]: "Has the LORD as great delight in burnt offerings and sacrifices, as in obeying the voice of the LORD? Behold, to obey is better than sacrifice, and to heed than the fat of rams. For rebellion is as the sin of witchcraft, and stubbornness is as iniquity and idolatry. Because you have rejected the word of the LORD, He also has rejected you from being king."
1 SAMUEL 15:22–23

But this is what I commanded them [the Israelites], saying, "Obey My voice, and I will be your God, and you shall be My people. And walk in all

203

the ways that I have commanded you, that it may be well with you." Yet they did not obey or incline their ear, but followed the counsels and the dictates of their evil hearts, and went backward and not forward.   JEREMIAH 7:23–24

[Jesus said,] "Not everyone who says to Me, 'Lord, Lord,' shall enter the kingdom of heaven, but he who does the will of My Father in heaven."
                                                MATTHEW 7:21

[Jesus said,] "But why do you call Me 'Lord, Lord,' and do not do the things which I say? Whoever comes to Me, and hears My sayings and does them, I will show you whom he is like: He is like a man building a house, who dug deep and laid the foundation on the rock. And when the flood arose, the stream beat vehemently against that house, and could not shake it, for it was founded on the rock. But he who heard and did nothing is like a man who built a house on the earth without a foundation, against which the stream beat vehemently; and immediately it fell. And the ruin of that house was great."   LUKE 6:46–49

[Be] obedient children, not conforming yourselves to the former lusts, as in your ignorance; but as He who called you is holy, you also be holy in all your conduct, because it is written, "Be holy, for I am holy."   1 PETER 1:14–16

Trusting and Obedient

Little children instinctively realize that they have to do nothing but obey their parents and leave everything else to them.

Likewise, we must realize the blessed fact that we have to do nothing but obey our Lord and leave everything else to His care.

Let us hear the conclusion of the whole matter: Fear God, and keep his commandments: for this is the whole duty of man.   ECCLESIASTES 12:13 KJV

[Jesus said,] "But seek first the kingdom of God and His righteousness, and all these things shall be added to you."   MATTHEW 6:33

THE PERFECT ROLE MODEL

Christ was the model of this divine childhood.

For unto us a Child is born, unto us a Son is given; and the government will be upon His shoulder. And His name will be called Wonderful, Counselor, Mighty God, Everlasting Father, Prince of Peace.
ISAIAH 9:6

He did nothing of Himself.

Then Jesus answered and said to them, "Most assuredly, I say to you, the Son can do nothing of Himself, but what He sees the Father do; for whatever He does, the Son also does in like manner."   JOHN 5:19

[Jesus said,] "I can of Myself do nothing. As I hear, I judge; and My judgment is righteous, because I do not seek My own will but the will of the Father who sent Me."   JOHN 5:30

He said nothing of Himself.

Then Jesus said to them, "When you lift up the Son of Man, then you will know that I am He, and that I do nothing of Myself; but as My Father taught Me, I speak these things."   JOHN 8:28

[Jesus said,] "He who rejects Me, and does not receive My words, has that which judges him; the word that I have spoken will judge him in the last day. For I have not spoken on My own authority; but the Father who sent Me gave Me a command, what I should say and what I should speak. And I know that His command is everlasting life. Therefore, whatever I speak, just as the Father has told Me, so I speak."   JOHN 12:48–50

Jesus walked in childlike obedience.

Then He went down with them [Joseph and Mary] and came to Nazareth, and was subject to them.
     LUKE 2:51

Jesus said to them, "My food is to do the will of Him who sent Me, and to finish His work."
     JOHN 4:34

[Jesus said,] "For I have come down from heaven, not to do My own will, but the will of Him who sent Me."   JOHN 6:38

Jesus referred everyone to His Father.

Then Jesus cried out and said, "He who believes in Me, believes not in Me but in Him who sent Me. And he who sees Me sees Him who sent Me."
     JOHN 12:44–45

Philip said to Him, "Lord, show us the Father, and it is sufficient for us." Jesus said to him, "Have I been with you so long, and yet you have not known Me, Philip? He who has seen Me has seen the Father; so how can you say, 'Show us the Father'?"
JOHN 14:8–9

Jesus said to them, "If God were your Father, you would love Me, for I proceeded forth and came from God; nor have I come of Myself, but He sent Me."
JOHN 8:42

Since Christ is our example, we must walk as He walked, with the spirit and ways of childhood.

For to this [suffering] you were called, because Christ also suffered for us, leaving us an example, that you should follow His steps.   1 PETER 2:21

He who says he abides in Him ought himself also to walk just as He walked.   1 JOHN 2:6

As a Little Child

Unless you...become as little children, you will by no means enter the kingdom of heaven.
MATTHEW 18:3

"As a little child, as a little child!
  Then how can I enter in?
I am scarred, and hardened, and soul-defiled,
  With traces of sorrow and sin.
Can I turn backward the tide of years
  And wake my dead youth at my will?"
"Nay, but thou canst, with thy grief and thy fears,
  Creep into My arms and be still."

"I know that the lambs in the heavenly fold
  Are sheltered and kept in Thy heart;
But I, I am old, and the gray from the gold
  Has bidden all brightness depart.
The gladness of youth, the faith and the truth,
  Lie withered or shrouded in dust."
"Thou art emptied at length of thy treacherous
    strength;
  Creep into My arms now, and trust."

"Is it true? Can I share with the little ones there
  A child's happy rest on Thy breast?"
"Aye, the tenderest care will answer thy prayer,
  My love is for thee as the rest.
It will quiet thy fears, will wipe away tears,
  Thy murmurs shall soften to psalms,
Thy sorrows shall seem but a feverish dream,
  In the rest, in the rest, of My arms.

"Thus tenderly held, the heart that rebelled,
  Shall cling to My hand, though it smite;
Shall find in My rod the love of its God,
  My statutes its songs in the night.
And whiter than snow shall the stained life grow,
  'Neath the touch of a love undefiled,
And the throngs of forgiven at the portals of heaven,
  Shall welcome one more little child."

Therefore whoever humbles himself as this little
child is the greatest in the kingdom of heaven.
MATTHEW 18:4